Presented to

_____

By

_____

Date

_____

My Favorite Bible Storybook™ for Early Readers

Published in 2005 by Spirit Press, an imprint of Dalmatian Press, LLC.

Copyright © 2005 Dalmatian Press, LLC

Written by Carolyn Larsen
Illustrated by Christopher Gray

The SPIRIT PRESS and MY FAVORITE BIBLE STORYBOOK
names and logos are trademarks of Dalmatian Press, LLC,
P.O. Box 682068, Franklin, Tennessee, 37067

ISBN: 1-40371-920-9 (X)

14746

Printed in China

06 07 08 09 CCO 10 9 8 7 6 5 4 3 2

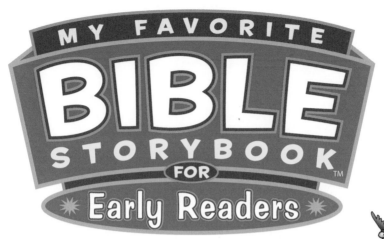

MY FAVORITE BIBLE STORYBOOK

FOR

✹ Early Readers ✹

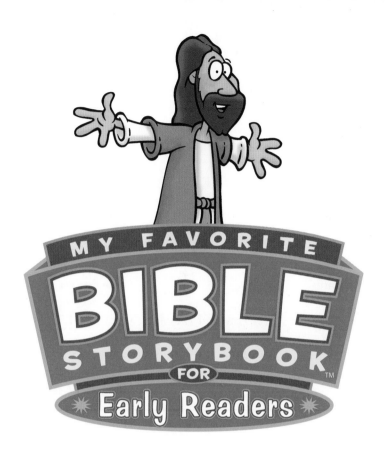

MY FAVORITE BIBLE STORYBOOK FOR Early Readers ™

Carolyn Larsen
Illustrated by **Christopher Grey**

SPIRIT PRESS

Table of Contents
Old Testament

New Testament

The Old Testament

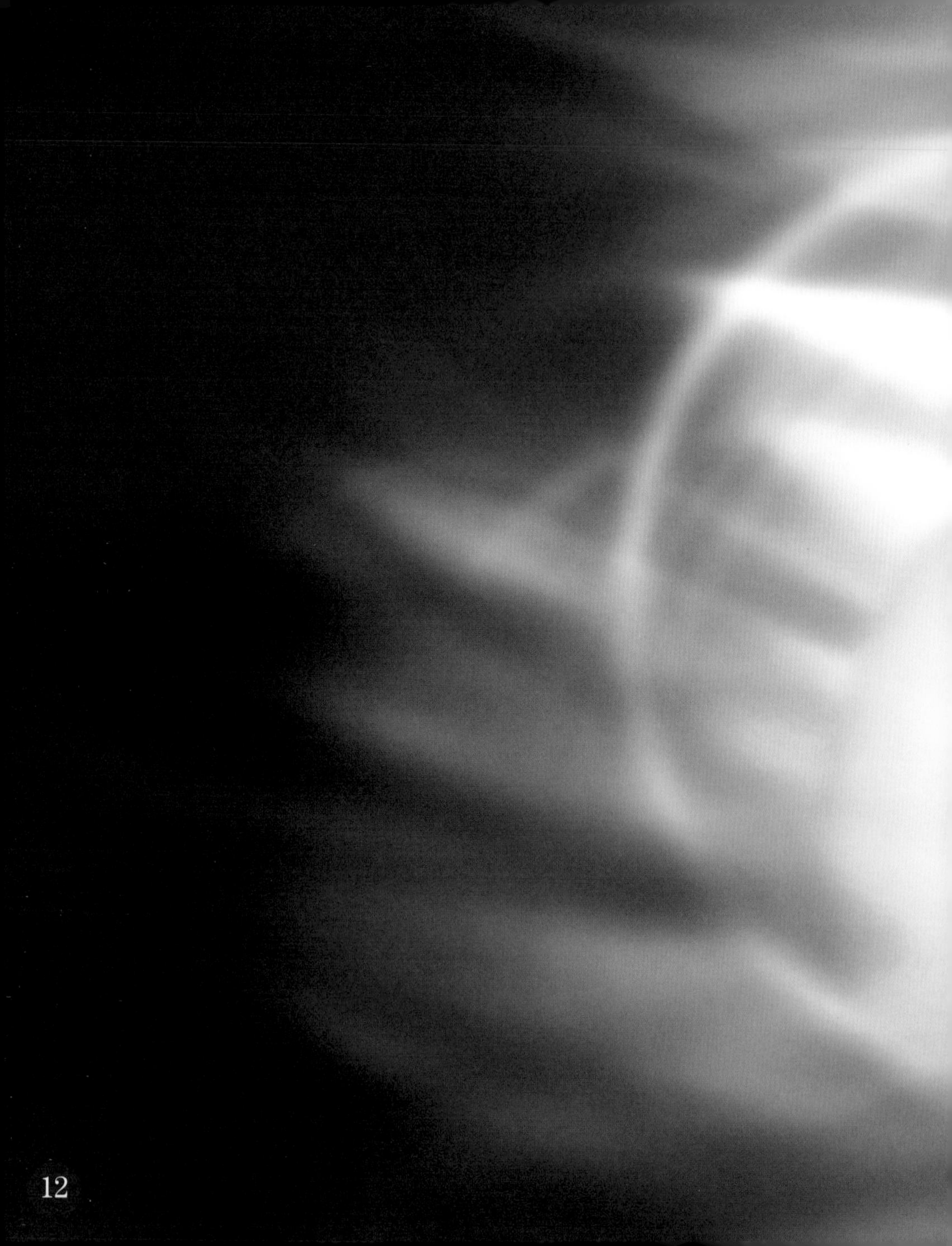

The Amazing Beginning

Genesis 1

In the very beginning, there was nothing. There were no oceans or mountains. There were no animals. There were no trees or flowers. There were no people alive anywhere. There was nothing but darkness. Then God began to create things.

All God had to do to make things was speak the words. He said, "Let there be light!" and the light shot through the darkness. God called the light "day." He called darkness "night." That was the end of His first day of work.

On His second day of creating,
God made the sky. It looked empty,
but God was preparing the earth for
the people, plants, and animals that
He was going to create. He made the
big, wonderful oceans on the
second day, too.

God made all of the plants on the third day. Big trees, small bushes, red flowers and purple ones. He filled the world with all the colors. He made rivers, seas and mountains, too. Beauty was everywhere.

His work on the fourth day was to make the sun, moon, and stars. On the fifth day of creation God made creatures that live in the oceans and all the birds that fly in the sky. That was a busy day!

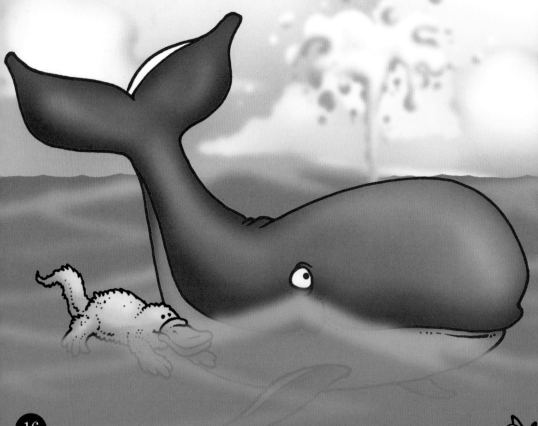

On the sixth day God made animals for the land. He thought of many different kinds. Little mice, big elephants, furry bears, and smooth zebras. The earth was filling up. But God had one more thing to make. It was something very special.

17

Fantastic Finish

Genesis 2

For six days God made things on the earth. He filled the earth with plants and animals. God liked the world He had made. Then God made one more thing before He stopped creating. It was His most amazing creation.

At the end of the sixth day, God
made the first man. Adam was made
in God's image. He could think. He
could make choices. He could talk
to God and obey Him. Adam
and God were friends.

God had an important job for Adam.
God marched all the animals past him.
Adam thought of a name for each one.
There were lots of animals.
He gave them names like
"butterfly" or "hippopotamus."

Adam finished naming the animals. He had many animals to play with or talk to. But Adam had no other person to be with. God knew it was not good for Adam to be alone. Adam needed a friend and helper. God knew what to do.

God made Eve, the
first woman. God took a
rib from Adam's body
and used it to make Eve.
Adam and Eve were very
happy together.

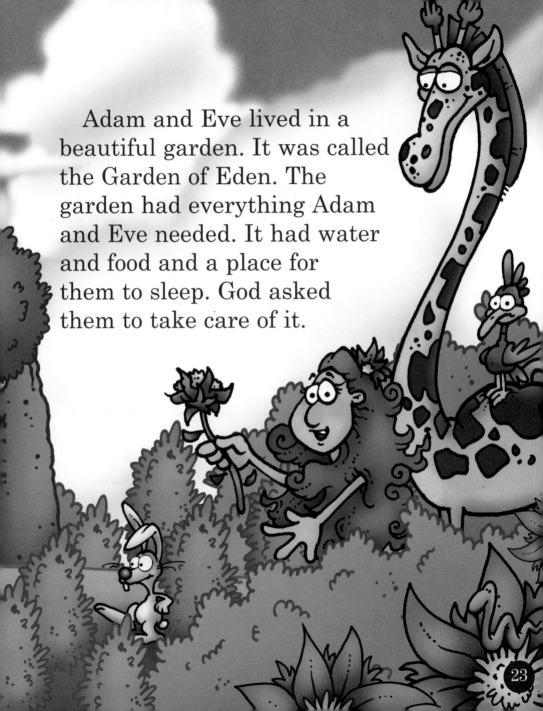

Adam and Eve lived in a beautiful garden. It was called the Garden of Eden. The garden had everything Adam and Eve needed. It had water and food and a place for them to sleep. God asked them to take care of it.

The First Bad Choice

Genesis 3

God made a beautiful garden. Adam and Eve, the first people, lived in it. He gave them one rule. They could eat fruit from any tree in the garden except one. If they touched the tree of the knowledge of good and evil, they would die.

One day Satan took on the shape of a snake and came to see Eve. "The fruit from the tree of the knowledge of good and evil is the best fruit in the garden," he said. "It will make you wise. Don't worry. God will not really punish you for eating it."

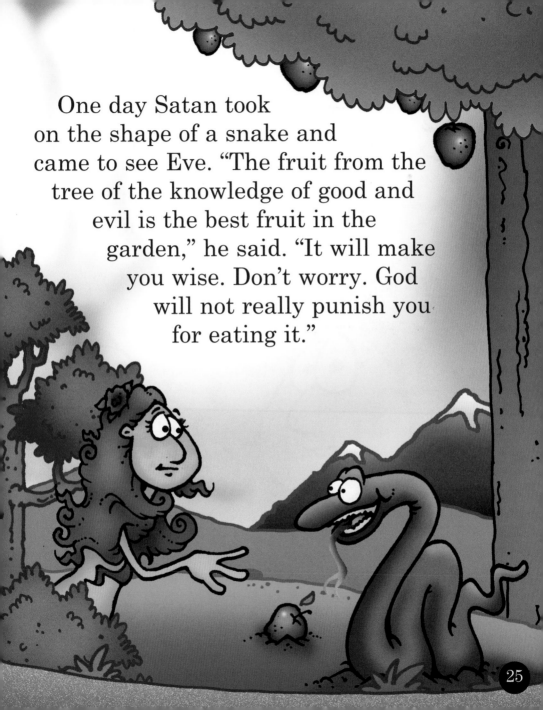

Eve thought the fruit from that tree looked juicy and sweet. So she decided to believe the snake. She pulled a piece of fruit from the tree and took a big bite.

Eve handed the fruit to
Adam and said, "Taste this."
Adam knew where the fruit had come
from. And he knew what God had said
about the fruit. But he took a big
bite anyway.

Adam and Eve knew they were in trouble. They had disobeyed God. They hid in the garden. They did not want to talk to God.

But God knew where Adam and Eve were hiding. He was sad because they disobeyed Him. He still loved them, but He had to punish them. God sent Adam and Eve out of the garden. God sent an angel to make sure they did not go back in the garden.

Obeying Pays Off

Genesis 6–9

Many years passed after Adam and Eve first disobeyed God. There were many people on earth now. But the people forgot all about God. They fought with each other. They were selfish and mean. Noah and his family were the only people who loved God.

God tried to get the people to remember Him. He wanted them to obey Him and love Him. But no one paid any attention to Him. God was sorry that He had even made people. He decided to empty the earth and start over.

God warned Noah about His plan. "A big, big flood is coming," He said. "I want you to build a really big boat—an ark. I will tell you exactly how to make it." God knew Noah would be safe in the ark.

Noah always tried to obey God. He got right to work measuring, hammering, and nailing. He built the ark just the way God told him. His neighbors made fun of him for building it. But Noah did not care. He just kept on working.

When the ark was finished, God sent animals to go inside it. He sent two of every kind of animal, a male and a female. He wanted them to be safe from the flood, too. Noah would make sure they had food and water.

The animals marched into the ark. Noah and his family went inside the ark, too. Then God Himself closed the big wooden door. Noah's friends and neighbors stood outside and laughed at him.

The Rainbow Promise

Genesis 7–9

After God shut the door of the ark, Noah and his family waited inside the ark. They waited and waited. Pretty soon they heard raindrops falling outside. It rained harder and harder. Before long they felt the ark start to float.

So much rain fell that the ground was covered with water. It kept on raining. The houses were covered with water. Soon even the trees and mountains were under water. Everything on earth was covered with water.

It rained for forty days and forty nights. Noah and the animals were safe and dry inside the ark. Finally the rain stopped. Noah waited for the water to go down a little. Then he sent out a raven to look for dry land. The bird did not find dry land.

Next, Noah sent out a dove. The dove came right back. There was still no dry land. Seven days later, Noah sent the dove out again. This time it brought back a leaf. A week later, Noah sent out the dove again. It did not come back. It had found dry land.

Noah waited a little while longer. He knew the water needed to go down some more. When he knew it was safe, Noah let all the animals out of the ark. They could run free again.

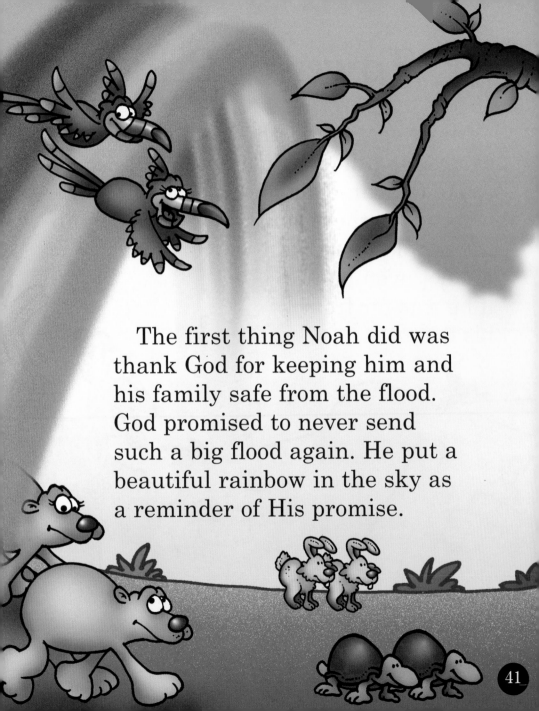

The first thing Noah did was thank God for keeping him and his family safe from the flood. God promised to never send such a big flood again. He put a beautiful rainbow in the sky as a reminder of His promise.

Tower of Pride

Genesis 11

Many years after the big flood, the earth was full of people again. All people spoke the same language. When a man went to another country, he could talk to the people there. It did not even matter if he was far from his home.

One day some men in Babel decided to build a tower. They planned to make it so tall that it would reach to heaven.

"Everyone will say that we are the greatest people who ever lived," they thought.

But God did not like their plan. He knew that they were building the tower because they were full of pride. He knew they thought they were more important than God. And He knew a way to stop them.

God made people start speaking different languages. They could not talk to each other any more. They could not work together. They could not finish the Tower of Babel.

No More Fighting!

Genesis 13

Many years after the Tower of Babel there lived a man named Abram. Abram was a man who obeyed God. God had blessed Abram. Abram owned large herds of cattle and sheep. He had lots of silver and gold, too.

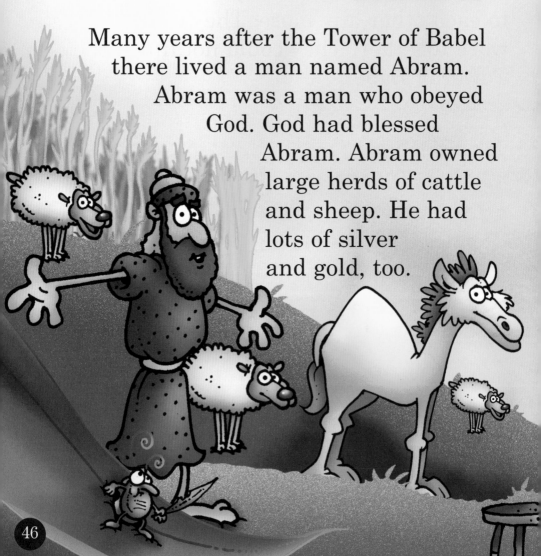

Abram's nephew, Lot, lived with him. God had also given Lot big herds of cattle and sheep.

As their crops and herds grew, a problem developed. Abram and Lot had so many cattle and sheep that there was not enough pasture land for all of them to find grass to eat.

The men who took care of the cattle and sheep started arguing. Abram's servants wanted enough food for their herd. Lot's servants wanted to be sure their sheep and cattle had food. Finally, Abram said, "The fighting must stop!"

Abram told Lot to choose where he wanted to live. Lot chose the land that had plenty of water and trees. Abram moved away. God said to him, "Look as far as you can see in every direction. I will give all this land to you. I will also give you children and grandchildren—too many to count!"

A Promise Named Laughter

Genesis 17–18, 21

Many years earlier, God had promised Abram, "You will have many children and grandchildren." God changed Abram's name to Abraham to remind him of this promise. But when Abraham was ninety-nine years old, he and his wife Sarah did not even have one child.

One day Abraham was
sitting outside his tent. God
came to visit in the form of three
men. The men were hot and tired.
Abraham invited them to sit down.
Abraham began talking with them.
God had something to
tell Abraham.

"Sarah," Abraham called, "make some dinner for our guests." Sarah cooked and listened while the men talked. Sarah made a good dinner. She served it to Abraham and the men. Then she went back inside to clean up.

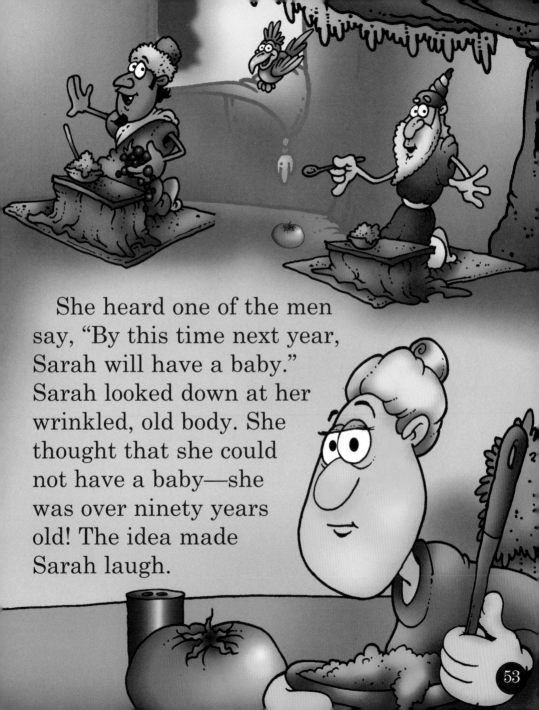

She heard one of the men say, "By this time next year, Sarah will have a baby." Sarah looked down at her wrinkled, old body. She thought that she could not have a baby—she was over ninety years old! The idea made Sarah laugh.

One of the men knew she was laughing. He said, "Is anything too hard for God? Do you think He cannot give you a baby?" Abraham did not know what to say.

About a year later, Sarah did have a baby boy. God kept His promise to Abraham and Sarah. God gave them a wonderful son. They named their baby boy Isaac because that name means "laughter."

Don't Look Back

Genesis 18–19

Abraham's nephew, Lot, and his family moved around many times. One place they moved to was a city called Sodom. It was not a good place for them. The people there did not love God.

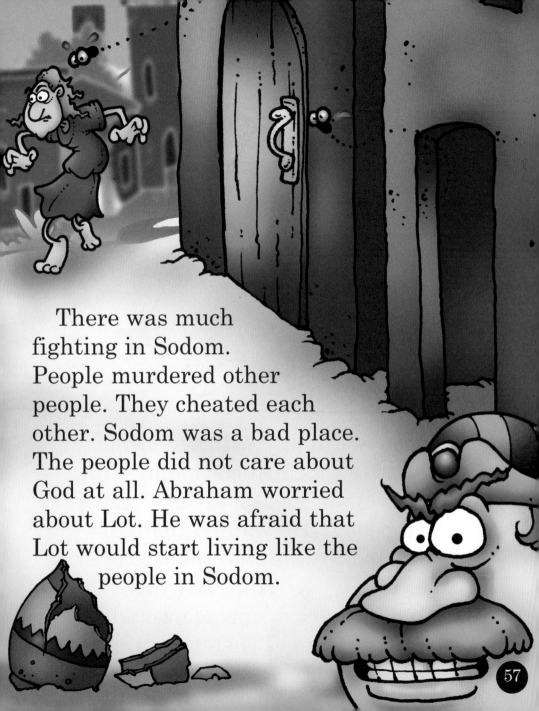

There was much fighting in Sodom. People murdered other people. They cheated each other. Sodom was a bad place. The people did not care about God at all. Abraham worried about Lot. He was afraid that Lot would start living like the people in Sodom.

57

God was not happy with the people in Sodom. He was also not happy with the people in another city, Gomorrah. He loved people. He wanted them to love Him, too. He wanted them to obey Him. But these people would not listen to Him.

Some of the men in Sodom tried to get Lot to do bad things with them. They tried to hurt Lot's daughters. God sent angels to protect Lot and his family. The men of Sodom tried to hurt the angels.

Finally, God was tired of the way the people were living. He decided to destroy Sodom and Gomorrah. Abraham begged God to let Lot escape. God sent two angels to Lot. "Leave the city," they said. "Run and do not look back." Lot and his family ran to the mountains.

Fire fell from heaven. Both cities burned. Lot's wife did not listen to what the angels said. She looked back at the cities. Her body turned into a statue of salt. Lot and his two daughters obeyed the angels. They were safe.

A Beautiful Bride

Genesis 24

Abraham and Sarah were very old when they had a son. The boy's name was Isaac. When Isaac was old enough to get married, Abraham did not want him to marry a girl from the country where they lived. The people there did not serve God.

Abraham had a plan to find a wife for Isaac. He called for his servant. "I want you to find a wife for Isaac," he told the man. "Go back to the land we came from. Find a wife for him there."

The servant took ten camels and left on the long trip. He was tired when he got to Abraham's country. He stopped by a well and prayed. He knew he needed God's help. The servant really wanted to find the right wife for Isaac.

After he prayed a young girl came up to him. She gave him a drink of water and said, "I will also get water for your camels." The servant had prayed that the girl God chose would say that very thing!

The girl's name was Rebekah. The servant gave her gifts. Then he asked if he could meet her family. She took the servant home to meet her family. The servant asked Rebekah's father if she could go back with him and marry Isaac.

Rebekah's father said yes. So she went with the servant. Isaac and Rebekah got married. Before long they were expecting their first baby. What a surprise when they had two babies—twin boys! They named them Jacob and Esau.

A Bad Trade

Genesis 25 & 27

Jacob and Esau were twin brothers. Their parents were Isaac and Rebekah. The brothers were not much alike. Jacob was a shepherd. He liked to do things at home. Esau liked to hunt. Jacob was his mother's favorite son. Isaac's favorite was Esau.

One day Esau went hunting as usual. He was gone all day. When he came home in the evening he was very hungry. Something smelled good in the house. Esau knew that Jacob had been cooking.

Sure enough, Jacob was standing by the fire, stirring a big pot of stew. Esau said, "Mmmm, that smells good. Let me have some." Jacob said, "Let's make a trade. I will give you stew. You give me your birthright."

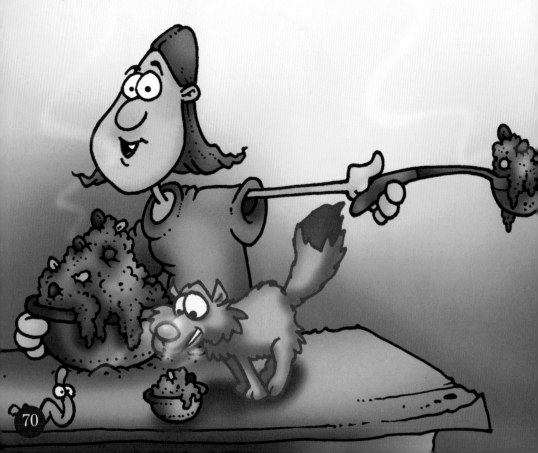

Whoever had the birthright would be the next leader in the family. The son with the birthright would get twice as much money when his father died. Jacob wanted Esau's birthright very much.

Jacob went right on stirring the stew. "Okay, I will give you my birthright," Esau said. "What good is it to have things if I starve to death?" That was just what Jacob wanted to hear.

Esau did not even stop to think about what he was doing. "I promise you my birthright," said Esau. So Jacob gave Esau a bowl of stew. Someday Esau would be sorry he had made this trade.

Family Tricks

Genesis 27

Isaac got old. He knew he was close to dying. He called his oldest son, Esau. "I am an old man," he said. "I will die soon. You were my firstborn son. I will give you my blessing and you will lead the family. Go hunting and bring back wild game for dinner. After I eat, I will bless you."

Rebekah heard what her husband said. She was angry. She wanted Jacob to get the blessing. He was her favorite son. She came up with a plan to steal the blessing for Jacob. Rebekah explained her plan to Jacob.

After Esau left,
Rebekah went to work.
She tied animal skins on
Jacob's arms. That made his
skin feel hairy like Esau's skin.
She wanted Isaac to think that
Jacob was Esau. Isaac could not
see very well. She was sure Jacob
could fool him.

Rebekah cooked her husband's favorite dinner. He would think the wild game he was eating was what Esau had brought home. Jacob put on some of Esau's clothes. Now he looked like Esau. He smelled like Esau, too.

Jacob took the food to his father.
Isaac thanked him and gave him a hug.
Jacob's arms felt like Esau's arms.
Isaac was fooled. He thought he was
talking to Esau. So he gave Jacob the
family blessing.

Esau came home later. He cooked a meal for Isaac and took it to him. Then they both realized what had happened. Esau begged his father for a blessing, too. Isaac was sad. But there was nothing he could do.

Happy Reunion

Genesis 32–33

Esau was angry with his brother. Jacob had stolen the family blessing from him. Their mother sent Jacob away until Esau calmed down. Jacob lived with his uncle. He took care of his uncle's sheep.

Jacob was gone a long time. He got married and had a family. But Jacob missed home. He wanted to go back to his own country. He even wanted to see his brother again. He wanted them to be friends again.

Jacob and his wife packed up their children. They set off for his country. They walked for a long time. Their servants and animals came, too. Jacob was happy to be going back to his family.

One day a servant came running to Jacob. "Esau is coming this way," the servant said. Jacob was scared. What if Esau was still mad at him? He was afraid for his family.

Jacob had gifts for Esau. He sent his servant to meet his brother on the road. "Give him these goats, sheep, camels, cattle, and donkeys. Tell him they are all from me," he said to the servant. "Tell him I am coming."

But Esau was not angry anymore. He did not even want Jacob's presents. He wanted to be friends with his brother again. He ran to his brother and hugged him. They both cried. Esau and Jacob were happy to be together again.

Green Monster of Jealousy

Genesis 37

Jacob had twelve sons. But they were not one big happy family. The problem was that Jacob liked one son more than the others. Joseph was his favorite. He gave Joseph special presents he did not give the other boys.

"Look at this colorful coat Father gave me!" Joseph said. It was the kind of coat that a rich man would wear. Young boys did not wear coats like that. Joseph's brothers were not happy for him. They were jealous of him.

One day Joseph told his brothers about a dream he had. "We were working in the field. We were gathering grain into bundles. All of a sudden your bundles bowed down to mine." Now Joseph's brothers were really mad at him.

Sometime later Joseph went to visit his brothers in the field where they were working. "Here comes Joseph," one brother said. "Let's kill him and tell Father that a wild animal ate him." But another brother said, "No, let's just throw him into a big hole and let him die there." So they did!

"Let me out!" Joseph begged. But his brothers just ignored him. Then one brother had a different idea. "See those men over there?" he said. "They are on their way to Egypt. Why don't we sell Joseph to them to be a slave?"

Soon Joseph was on his way to Egypt. His brothers told their father that a wild animal had killed him. Joseph did not know what was going to happen to him. But he knew that God would take care of him.

91

Making the Best of a Bad Situation

Genesis 39–41

A man named Potiphar bought Joseph to be his slave. Joseph worked hard for his owner. But Potiphar's wife wanted to get Joseph in trouble. She told her husband a lie about Joseph. Potiphar became so angry at Joseph that he threw him in jail.

Joseph met another prisoner. This man once worked for Pharaoh, the ruler of Egypt. One night that man had a dream. God helped Joseph explain the dream. It meant that the man would be free soon. "Remember me," Joseph said. He wanted to get out of prison, too. The man *was* freed, but he forgot all about Joseph.

Then one night Pharaoh had a dream. He dreamed that there were seven fat, healthy cows eating grass. Seven skinny, sick cows came up and ate the healthy cows. He did not understand what the dream meant.

Pharaoh had
another dream.
In this dream,
there were seven fat,
healthy heads of grain
growing on a stalk.
Seven skinny heads
of grain grew up on
the same stalk. They
swallowed up the good grain.
He did not understand this
dream either.

Pharaoh called for his wise men. "What do my dreams mean?" he asked. They did not know. Then the man who had been in prison remembered Joseph. He told Pharaoh that Joseph understood dreams. Pharaoh sent for Joseph.

"Your dreams mean that Egypt will have seven good years. There will be lots of food. After that there will be seven bad years when there will be no food," Joseph said. Pharaoh was happy to know what his dreams meant. He gave Joseph an important job in the country.

97

The Forgiving Brother

Genesis 42–46

Pharaoh, ruler of Egypt, was very happy when God helped Joseph explain his dreams. He took Joseph out of prison and made him second in command over all of Egypt. Joseph ordered that food and grain be stored in warehouses during the good years. He knew they would need that food when the bad years came.

Sure enough, the bad years came. It did not rain. It was very hot. No food would grow anywhere. People in other countries were starving to death. But in Egypt there was plenty of food because of Joseph's good planning.

People from other countries heard about the food in Egypt. They came to buy food. One day some men from Canaan came. The men were Joseph's brothers! They had sold him to be a slave many years before.

Joseph's brothers bowed down to him. As a boy, Joseph had once had a dream about this very day. Joseph knew they were his brothers. He sold them some food, but he did not tell them who he was. They did not recognize him.

The brothers took the food home to their father. When they needed more food, they came back to Egypt. They bowed down to Joseph again and asked him to sell them more food. This time, Joseph told them that he was their brother.

His brothers were afraid Joseph would put them in prison. "Do not be afraid," Joseph said. "I know you meant to hurt me a long time ago. But God turned what you did into good." Then Joseph asked his whole family to move to Egypt so he could take care of them.

A Floating Crib

Exodus 1, 2

After Joseph died, his family remained in Egypt and grew into a large nation, known as the Hebrews. A new Pharaoh was ruling Egypt. He did not remember how much help Joseph had been. He just worried there were too many Hebrews. So Pharaoh ordered that all Hebrew baby boys be killed.

One mother decided to hide her baby boy. She hid him until he was too big to hide anymore. His cries were too loud. She was scared that the soldiers would hear him. The mother came up with a plan to save her son.

She made a basket from long pieces of grass. She put her baby inside the basket and floated it on the river. Then the woman went home. The baby's older sister stayed to watch the basket.

Pretty soon, Pharaoh's daughter came to the river. She saw the basket floating by and asked a servant to bring it to her. She was surprised to find a little Hebrew baby inside. She thought he was cute.

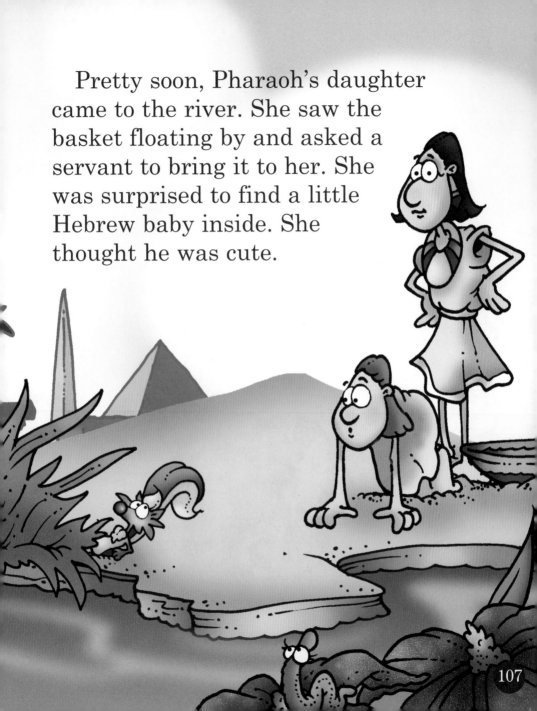

The baby's sister watched from her hiding place. She saw that the princess wanted to keep the baby. She asked the princess if she wanted her to find a Hebrew woman to be the nurse. The princess said yes. The little girl got the baby's own mother to be the nurse!

The brave Hebrew mother saved her little boy. She got to take care of him and teach him about God. That little boy was Moses. He grew up in the palace as a prince.

Hot Topics

Exodus 3 & 4

Moses grew up as the adopted son of the Egyptian princess. But his family and people, the Hebrews, were slaves in Egypt. One day Moses saw an Egyptian beating a Hebrew slave. Moses killed the Egyptian and buried him in the sand. Pharaoh heard about it and commanded that Moses be arrested. Moses was forced to leave Egypt. He ran away to Midian where he became a shepherd.

One day Moses was watching his sheep. Suddenly, he saw a bush that was on fire. It kept burning, but it did not burn up. God spoke to him from the burning bush. "Moses, I want you to lead My people out of Egypt. Tell Pharaoh to let My people go," God said.

Moses was afraid. He did not think he could do this job. God knew that he was afraid. He said, "I will help you do this job. I want My people to have their own land."

Moses was still afraid.

"Throw down your rod," God said. Moses did. It became a snake. "Pick it up," God said. Moses did and it became a rod again. "I will do miracles like this to show that I am with you," God said. Moses agreed to do what God wanted.

God's Warnings
Exodus 5–11

Moses returned to Egypt where he was born. He went to Pharaoh and said, "God says, 'Let My people go.'" Pharaoh would not. So God performed a miracle to show His mighty power.

He turned all the water in Egypt into blood. But Pharaoh would not listen to Moses.

God then sent frogs to cover the land. Frogs were everywhere, except where the Hebrew people lived. They were in beds and in dishes. "Make the frogs go away and I will let the Hebrews leave," Pharaoh said. But when the frogs were gone, he would not let them leave.

God sent small flies all over Egypt. They flew into people's mouths and eyes. But Pharaoh still did not let the people leave. Then God sent millions of bigger flies. They bit the Egyptian people and animals. Nothing happened to the Hebrews. The stubborn Pharaoh still said, "The people cannot go."

Next, all the animals in Egypt got very sick. But Pharaoh still did not let the Hebrews go. Then God made the Egyptian people get painful sore spots all over their bodies. That did not change Pharaoh's mind either.

Next, a hailstorm ruined the Egyptians' ripe crops. Pharaoh still refused to let the Hebrews leave. Grasshoppers ate the young crops. "Go," Pharaoh said. But he was lying. God made the sun stop shining. But Pharaoh still did not change his mind.

What God did last was the most terrible. The oldest son in each Egyptian family died. Even the Pharaoh's son died. Pharaoh said "Go!" one more time. This time he meant it. Moses led the Hebrew people out of Egypt.

No Muddy Feet Here!

Exodus 14–15

God told Moses to lead the Hebrew people out of Egypt. The people walked out of Egypt and God was with them. A big moving fire led them in the nighttime. It changed to a cloud in the daytime.

The Hebrew people walked and walked. Finally, they came to the edge of the Red Sea. "Let's camp here," Moses said. So the people unpacked and set up their tents. They were tired.

Back in Egypt, Pharaoh changed his mind again. He wanted the Hebrews back. He sent his army after them. The Hebrews saw a cloud of dust in the distance. It was far away, but it was coming closer. It was the Egyptian army.

"Moses, what are we going to do?" the people cried. The Red Sea was in front of them. The army was behind them. They were trapped. "Do not be afraid," Moses said. "God will take care of us."

Then God created another miracle. He pushed part of the water of the Red Sea back one way. He pushed the rest of the water back the other way. He made a dry path across the seafloor. The people walked through the Red Sea with big walls of water on each side.

Manna from Heaven

Exodus 16

Moses and the Hebrew people had walked in the desert for over a month. They were happy to no longer be slaves in Egypt. But now they were hungry. They could not find much food in the desert.

"We want food!" the people cried. "We should have stayed in Egypt," they said to Moses. "At least we had food there."

"What if we starve to death out here in the desert?" someone asked.

Some of them were angry that Moses had taken them out of Egypt. They forgot about being slaves and the hard work they had been forced to do.

God heard the people groaning. He wanted to help them. He did not want them to starve. God knew what to do. He explained to Moses exactly what He would do.

The next morning there were strange white flakes on the ground. "What is this?" the people asked. "It is food from heaven," Moses said. "God sent it for you." The people called the food "manna." They thanked God for taking care of them.

Ten Good Rules
Exodus 19–20

One night, after the Hebrews had
been walking for three months, they
stopped to camp near Mount Sinai.
They were getting settled when
God called Moses to come up
onto the mountain.

God told Moses some important things to pass on to the people. Moses told everyone, "Be ready for the third day!" Three days later the earth shook as if there were an earthquake. The sky got dark as night. Thunder crashed and lightning zigzagged across the sky. God showed His power.

Moses climbed the mountain again to meet with God. The light of God filled Moses, and his hair turned white. Then God wrote special rules for the people on pieces of stone. Some of the rules would help the people live for God. They should worship God only. They should not use God's name in a bad way. They should rest on God's day.

The other rules would help them get along with others. They should honor their parents. They should not murder. Married people should be faithful to each other. People should not steal. They should not lie. They should not want things that belong to others.

Moses brought the rules to the people. "We will obey them," the people said.

The Marching Army

Joshua 1–2, 6

Moses led the Hebrew people for many years while they walked through the desert. When Moses died, God chose Joshua to be the new leader. He was strong and brave. The people were still waiting for the land God had promised to give them.

One day God spoke to
Joshua. He told him to get
his soldiers ready. "In three
days we will go into the land God
promised us," Joshua told them.

"We will do whatever you tell us," the
soldiers said. "We will obey you just as
we obeyed Moses." Then Joshua
asked two soldiers to go spy
on the city of Jericho.

The spies sneaked into the city of Jericho. At night they came to the home of a woman named Rahab. They spent the night there. But someone saw them and told the king, and he sent soldiers to find them. Rahab hid them on the roof of her house. The soldiers did not find them.

"I helped you, so will you let me live with your people?" Rahab asked. She had heard how God helped the Hebrew people. The spies told her to hang a red rope in her window. The red rope would help them find her quickly when they came back to the city.

God told Joshua exactly what He wanted the Hebrew people to do to capture Jericho. For six days the Hebrew people marched around the city once a day. Some priests blew their horns. No one shouted. No one said a word. They did just what God said.

On the seventh day, the Hebrew people marched around the city seven times. Then the priests blew a long note on their horns. "Shout!" Joshua yelled. "God has given us Jericho!" The soldiers shouted as loud as they could.

The big, thick walls around the city began to crack and crumble. Then they crashed to the ground. Joshua's soldiers rushed in to the city. God had given the Hebrew people this city. He kept His promise.

The two men who had been spies hurried to find Rahab's house. They looked for the red rope hanging in the window. When they found Rahab, they kept their promise. Rahab and her family lived with the Hebrews after that.

The Strongest Man

Judges 13–14, 16

Other nations heard how God helped the Hebrew people, also called the Israelites. One army, the Philistines, captured the Israelites and ruled them for forty years. During that time an angel spoke to one Israelite woman. "God will give you a son. He will become a Nazarite. Do not cut his hair. Long hair will be a sign that he serves God."

The Israelite woman gave birth to a son named Samson. Samson lived for God and grew into a very strong man. Word of his strength spread when he defeated some Philistine men. The Philistines hated him. Once, they tried to capture him in the town of Gaza. But Samson tore the city gates right out of the ground and escaped.

The Philistines went to a woman named Delilah, who knew Samson. They asked her to find out what made Samson so strong. They would pay her lots of money if she could find out. If they knew how to make him weak, they could trick him and capture him.

Delilah begged Samson to tell her
where his strength came from. "Tie me
up with new ropes," he said. "I will be
weak and unable to get away."
When he fell asleep, she tied him
up with new ropes. But
Samson woke and broke
the ropes as if they were
strings.

Delilah shouted at Samson for lying to her. Finally he said, "If my hair is cut, I will be no stronger than anyone else." When he fell asleep, Delilah called in the Philistines to shave Samson's hair. He woke up and foughtthem, but his strength was gone and they captured him.

After some
time had passed, the
Philistines had a party to
celebrate capturing Samson. The
people laughed at Samson and
made fun of him.

"God, help me one more time,"
Samson prayed. God did! Samson
pushed on the big pillars that held
up the roof. It crashed down and
killed the Philistines.

Loyal Ruth

Ruth 1–4

Many years after Samson died, a drought struck the land of Judah. No food grew and rivers dried up. People starved to death. Naomi and Elimelech lived in Judah. They were worried that their two sons would die. They moved away from their family to the land of Moab. There was plenty of food there.

The boys grew up and married girls from Moab. Life went well until Naomi's husband died. She was so sad. Things got even harder when her sons died, too. Now Naomi only had her two daughters-in-law, Orpah and Ruth. She became lonely for her family back in Judah.

149

Naomi decided to go home to Judah. Ruth wanted to go with her. She said, "I will go where you go. Your people will be my people. Your God will be my God." Naomi tried to talk her into staying in Moab. But Ruth wanted to go. She was loyal to Naomi.

Naomi and Ruth settled in Judah. Ruth took care of her mother-in-law. She made sure they had food. Ruth walked behind the workers in the fields. She picked up any grain they dropped. Then she made bread from it. It was hard work, but they were happy. God was watching over them.

Boaz was the owner of the fields where Ruth worked. He saw how hard Ruth worked to take care of Naomi. He told the workers to leave extra grain in the field for Ruth.

Ruth and Boaz fell in love and got married. Soon they had a baby boy. His name was Obed. Ruth, Boaz, Obed, and Naomi were very happy. God had taken good care of Naomi and Ruth.

Bigger Is Not Better

1 Samuel 17

God chose a young man named Saul to be king. King Saul went to war against the Philistines. One Philistine soldier named Goliath was nine feet tall! Every day for forty days Goliath shouted for someone to come and fight him. King Saul and his army did nothing. They were scared.

Jesse's son David, the shepherd boy, came to visit his brothers. They were soldiers in King Saul's army. As soon as he got there, David heard Goliath making fun of King Saul's army. "Who is this man?" David asked. "Why is he saying these things about God's people?"

David wasn't scared. "I will fight the giant," he told King Saul. All David had to fight with was a slingshot. Goliath had a big, sharp spear and a full set of armor. "God will help me," David said. He knew that he could not lose!

King Saul's soldiers watched as little David marched away. He stopped and picked up five smooth stones for his slingshot. Goliath saw him coming. He was angry that a young boy was coming to fight him.

"Come on, kid! I will feed you to the birds!" Goliath shouted.

"I'm not scared of you. God will help me win," David called back. "This battle is the Lord's." He put a stone in his slingshot. He swung it around. Then he let go and the stone flew through the air.

SMACK! The stone hit Goliath right on the head. The big giant crashed to the ground. Because David trusted God, God helped David win. King Saul's soldiers cheered! The Philistine army ran away!

Music for the Heart
1 Samuel 16; Psalms

God chose David to be the new king of Israel. King Saul was angry about that. He chased David but God protected David. David did become king after Saul died. He was a good king. He loved God.

David wrote songs about his love for God. He wrote, "I will thank You, LORD, with all my heart. I will tell of all the marvelous things You have done. I will be filled with joy because of You. I will sing praises to Your Name, O Most High."

David trusted God. He wrote, "You are my Master! All the good things I have are from You! I am praying to You because I know You will answer, O God. As for God, His way is perfect. All the LORD's promises prove true. He is a shield for all who look to Him for protection."

"Shout with joy to the LORD, O earth. Worship the LORD with gladness. Come before Him, singing with joy. Acknowledge that the LORD is God! He made us, and we are His. We are His people, the sheep of His pasture."

Solomon's Good Choice

1 Kings 3

King David had a son named Solomon. When he grew up, Solomon became king of Israel. He obeyed God. He led the people to obey God, too.

One night God came to Solomon in a dream. God said He would give Solomon anything he wanted.

Solomon said, "You have been so kind to me. Now I am king, but I don't know how to be a king." Then he asked God to give him wisdom. "I want to be a good king. I want to know right from wrong."

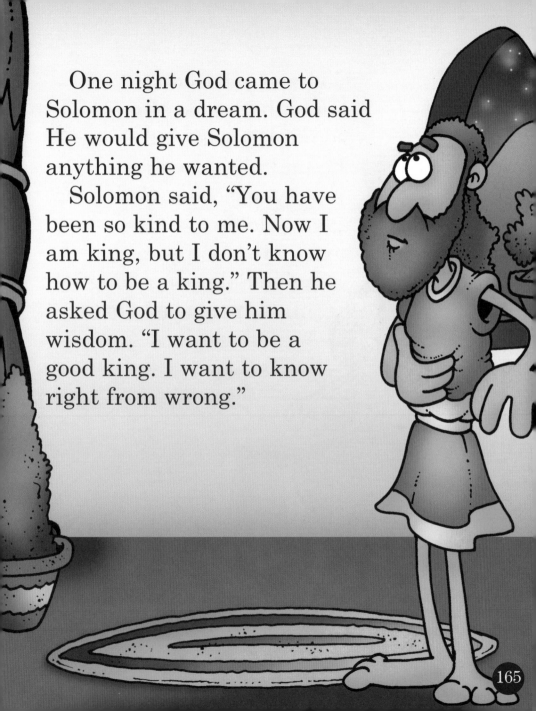

God was pleased that
Solomon had asked for
wisdom. He was glad that
he had not asked for
money or power. God
gave Solomon a wise
heart. He also promised
to give Solomon a long
life if he obeyed God.

Wise King Solomon solved many people's problems. Once there were two women who lived in the same house and were about the same age. One woman's son had died during the night. That woman stole the other woman's living son. She left her dead son in his place.

Both women told Solomon, "The living baby is my son." Solomon had to decide which woman was telling the truth. He called for a servant to bring a sword. He ordered the servant to cut the living baby in half and give one part to each mother.

One woman shouted, "No! Do not hurt the baby. Let this other woman have him." Now King Solomon knew that the woman who had shouted was the real mother. Only a real mother would give up her baby rather than have him hurt. God made Solomon a wise man.

A Home for God

1 Kings 5–8

God gave Solomon the gift of wisdom. News of Solomon's wisdom spread through the land and even to other countries. People came from all over to ask the king's advice on many things. God also gave him money and power.

King Solomon wanted to build a special house for God. He wanted the people to be able to come there to worship God. It would be beautiful. It would honor God.

The king needed many workers to build the temple. Some worked with stone. Some worked with wood. One man made beautiful things for the inside of the temple. The walls inside were covered with gold.

It took seven years to build the temple. When it was finished, Solomon called the people together. "Dear God, thank You for Your goodness and kindness," he prayed. The people had a big party to thank God for His help.

Queen Esther's Courage

Esther 1–10

The king of Persia was looking for a new queen. He wanted her to be very beautiful. He held a contest and lots of girls came. They stayed together and were given special food. The king's servants helped them to get ready for the contest. They all wanted to look their best for the king.

One girl stood out above all the others. Her name was Esther. She was very beautiful. She was also sweet and kind to everyone. When the king saw her, he knew that she was the right girl to be queen. He fell in love with her.

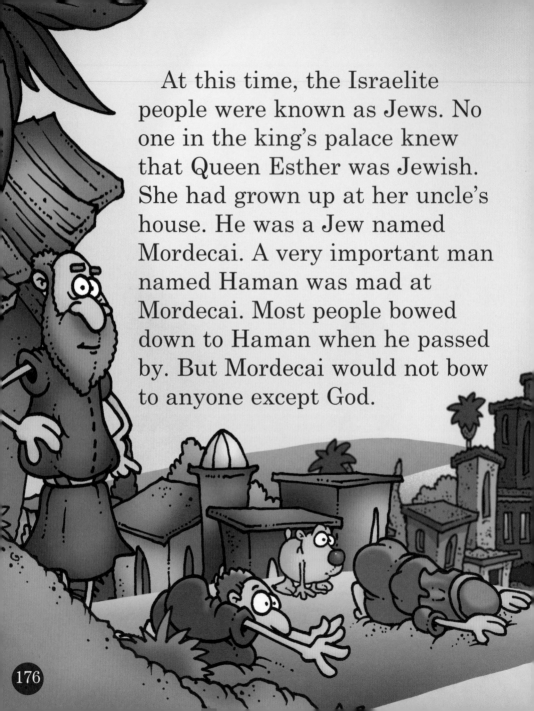

At this time, the Israelite people were known as Jews. No one in the king's palace knew that Queen Esther was Jewish. She had grown up at her uncle's house. He was a Jew named Mordecai. A very important man named Haman was mad at Mordecai. Most people bowed down to Haman when he passed by. But Mordecai would not bow to anyone except God.

Haman decided to have all the Jews in the land killed because of Mordecai. He tricked the king into signing a new law. Now Haman could give orders to kill all the Jews in the land. Still no one knew that Queen Esther was Jewish.

Mordecai came to Esther and begged her to help the Jews. She decided to have a special dinner just for the king and Haman. As they ate, the king told Esther that he would do anything for her. So Esther told him about Haman's plan to kill the Jews. She also told the king that she was Jewish, so she would be killed, too.

The king was very angry. He had guards take Haman outside. He commanded that Haman be hanged. Haman was hanged on the same platform he had built to kill Mordecai. Thanks to brave Queen Esther the Jews were saved!

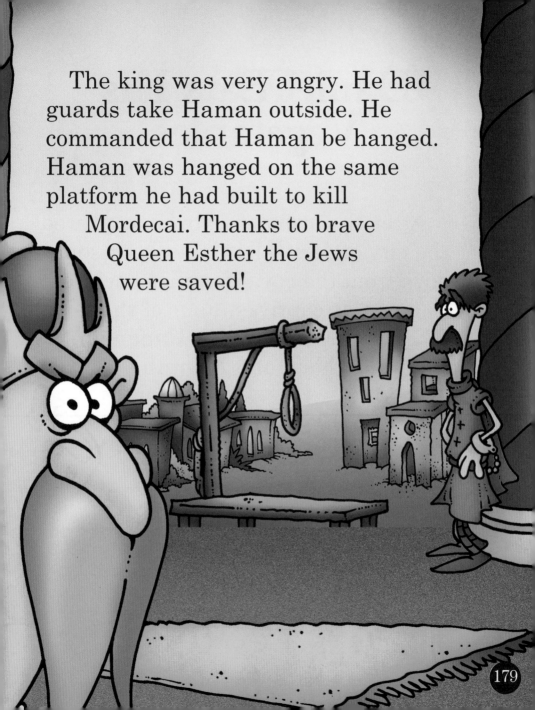

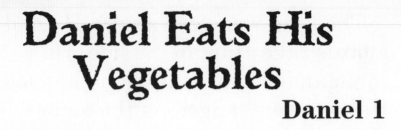

Daniel Eats His Vegetables

Daniel 1

After the army of Babylon captured the city of Jerusalem, they took some boys from the royal families back to Babylon as captives. Four of those boys were Daniel, Hananiah, Mishael, and Azariah.

The king called these boys Belteshazzar, Shadrach, Meshach, and Abednego. They were put into a special training program in the king's palace with a few other boys. He gave them special food. It was the same food that was served to the king. This food was better than the food the other slaves were given.

Daniel knew that the king's food was not good for them to eat. It had been offered to idols. Eating it would be like honoring the idols instead of God. Daniel thought of a plan and went to talk to the guard. "Please let us eat vegetables and water instead of the king's food," he said.

The guard said, "No. If you eat only vegetables and water, you will not be as healthy as the other boys." The guard would be in trouble if the boys were not healthy. He might be killed.

"Just let us try my plan for ten days," Daniel said. "Then, if we are not as healthy as the others, you can decide what to do." Daniel's plan seemed safe to the guard. He agreed to let the boys try it.

The test time ended. The guard checked on Daniel and his friends. They were healthier than all of the other boys who were still eating the king's food. The guard let them keep eating vegetables and water. God helped Daniel and his friends make a good decision.

The Fiery Furnace

Daniel 3

The king of Babylon thought he was very important. He made a big statue of himself out of pure gold. He wanted all the people to worship it. "When you hear music play, fall to your knees and worship my statue," he said.

All the people in the land listened for the horns to blow. When they heard the music, they bowed to the statue. But Shadrach, Meshach, and Abednego would not bow down to the statue. They would not worship anyone or anything except God.

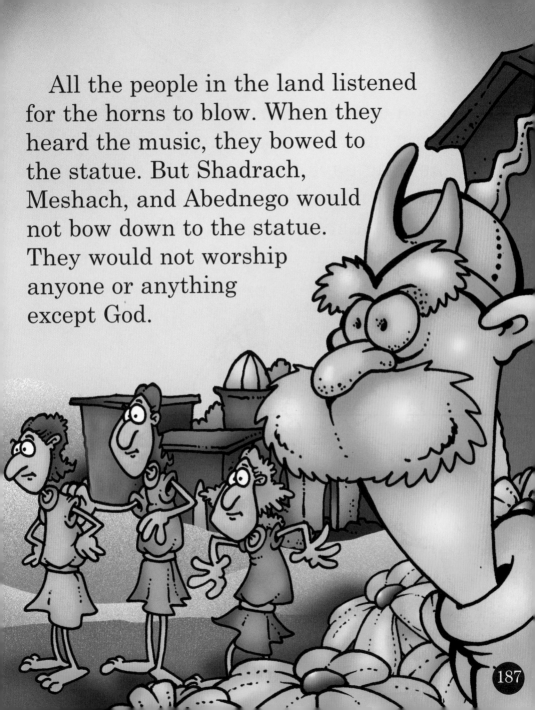

Some soldiers grabbed the three young men and took them to the king. The king gave them another chance to bow down to the statue. "We will never worship a statue," they said. "Punish us if you want. We know God will take care of us."

The king was very angry.
"Heat up the fire in the furnace.
Make it seven times hotter
than it usually is!" he ordered.
"Now tie up these men and
throw them into the fire." The
fire was so hot that the
soldiers who
threw them
in were
killed.

The king watched, but he could not believe what he saw! The three men were walking around in the fire. There was a fourth man with them, too. He looked like an angel. "Come here!" the king called. The men came out of the fire.

They were not burned at all. They did not even smell like smoke. The king said, "These men were willing to die rather than worship another god." Then he praised God. He even said that everyone should praise Him.

Lions and Angels

Daniel 6

Daniel was a slave in Babylon, but the king liked him very much. God made Daniel wise. He helped Daniel make good decisions. The king made Daniel a ruler in his government. Daniel did a good job for many years. The king planned to give him an even more important job.

However, some bad men were jealous of Daniel. They looked for a way to get him in trouble. But since Daniel was a good man, he did not do bad things. They knew he obeyed God. They knew he prayed to God every day. That gave them an idea.

The men went to the king. "You should sign a law that people in the land can pray only to you," they said. "If anyone disobeys this law, he will be thrown into the lions' den." The king liked their idea. He did not know they were tricking him.

Daniel heard about the law. But he kept right on praying to God. Daniel obeyed God no matter what. The bad men spied on Daniel. When they saw him praying, they rushed to tell the king. They demanded that the king punish him.

The king was sad. He knew now
that he had been tricked. The king
had to throw Daniel into the lions' den
because that was the law. The king said,
"May your God save you!"
All night the king
worried about Daniel.
He did not eat. He did
not sleep.

Early the next morning the king ran to see what had happened to Daniel. God had protected him! The lions had not even touched him. Daniel praised God. The king also praised God for keeping Daniel safe.

A Fishy Trip

Jonah 1–4

Some years after Jeremiah lived, Jonah served God as a prophet. God had a special job for Jonah. "Go to Nineveh," He said. "The people there are doing bad things. I want you to tell them to stop."

Jonah decided not to obey God. He thought he could run away from God. Jonah got on a boat that was sailing away from Nineveh. He went to a room in the bottom part of the ship. He fell asleep there.

But God knew where Jonah was. He sent a big storm. The boat bounced around on the waves. The sailors were afraid their boat was going to sink. They woke Jonah. "If you believe in God, you had better pray. We may drown in this bad storm," they told Jonah.

Jonah knew that he was the reason for the storm. "Throw me overboard and the storm will stop," he told the sailors. They did not want to toss Jonah into the sea. But they did want the storm to stop. So they did what Jonah asked and threw him into the stormy sea.

The storm stopped. The
sailors thought Jonah
would drown. But God sent
a big fish that swallowed Jonah
right up. Jonah lived inside the fish
for three days. He had plenty of time
to think about how he had
disobeyed God.

Jonah prayed, "I'm sorry for disobeying. If You let me live, I will go to Nineveh." The big fish spat Jonah out on the shore. Then Jonah headed right for Nineveh. He told the people to stop doing bad things. They listened to Jonah and started obeying God.

The New Testament

His Name Is John

Luke 1

Zechariah was a priest in the temple. He loved God. So did his wife, Elizabeth. They obeyed God. They did not have any children, even though they had always wanted to be parents. Now they were too old to have a baby.

One day
Zechariah was
alone in the
temple.
Suddenly
he heard a
voice say,
"God sent me to give
you some good news.
You and your
wife will have a
baby boy. You
must name him
John. He will be
God's servant. He
will bring people
back to God."

Zechariah asked, "How
do I know that what you
say is true?"

The angel said, "I am
Gabriel. I come from
God. Since you do not
believe me, you will
not be able to speak
until the baby is
born. Everything will
happen just as I
have said."

After that Zechariah could not speak at all. When he came out of the temple, he made signals with his hands. He tried to tell people that he had seen an angel. He could not even tell his wife about the angel.

A few months later, Elizabeth was expecting a baby. Things were happening just as the angel said they would. Friends and family celebrated with the happy couple. When the baby was born, people said, "Name him after his father."

But Elizabeth said, "We will name him John."

"Why would you name him that? No one in your family has that name," the people said. They asked Zechariah what he thought. He grabbed a tablet and wrote, "His name is John." Right away Zechariah's voice came back! The first thing he did was praise God.

The Angel's Announcement

Luke 1

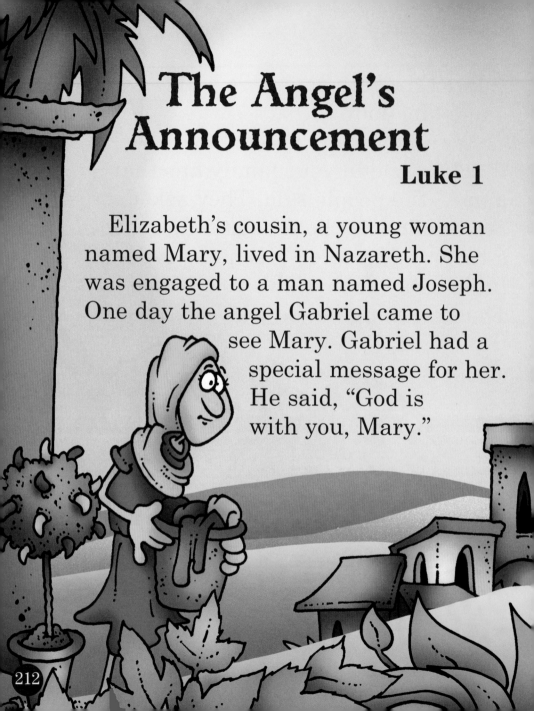

Elizabeth's cousin, a young woman named Mary, lived in Nazareth. She was engaged to a man named Joseph. One day the angel Gabriel came to see Mary. Gabriel had a special message for her. He said, "God is with you, Mary."

Mary was confused. She did not know what the angel meant.

"Do not be afraid," Gabriel said. "God loves you and He is pleased with you. You are going to have a baby. God wants you to name Him Jesus. He will be God's Son!"

Mary was even more confused now. "How can I have a baby? I am not even married," she said.

"Nothing is impossible with God," Gabriel said. "Your baby will be the holy Son of God. He will rule the people."

"I am the Lord's servant," Mary said. "I believe what you are telling me. I will do whatever God wants." Gabriel left then. In a short time Mary was expecting a baby, just as Gabriel had said.

The angel's news confused Joseph, too. But he and Mary trusted God, and soon they were married.

A Special Night

Luke 1–2

Mary and Joseph had to make a long trip. The king wanted to know how many people he could tax. Every man returned to the town he came from, and brought his family to be counted. Mary and Joseph traveled seventy miles to Bethlehem. The trip was hard on Mary because she was going to have a baby soon.

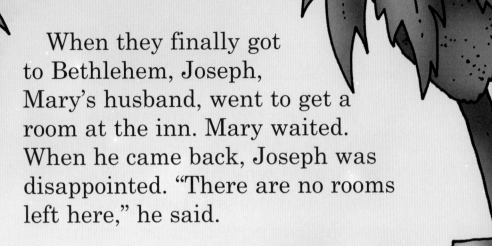

When they finally got
to Bethlehem, Joseph,
Mary's husband, went to get a
room at the inn. Mary waited.
When he came back, Joseph was
disappointed. "There are no rooms
left here," he said.

"We can stay in the stable with the animals," Joseph said. The stable was full of animal smells and noises. But it was a good place to rest for the night.

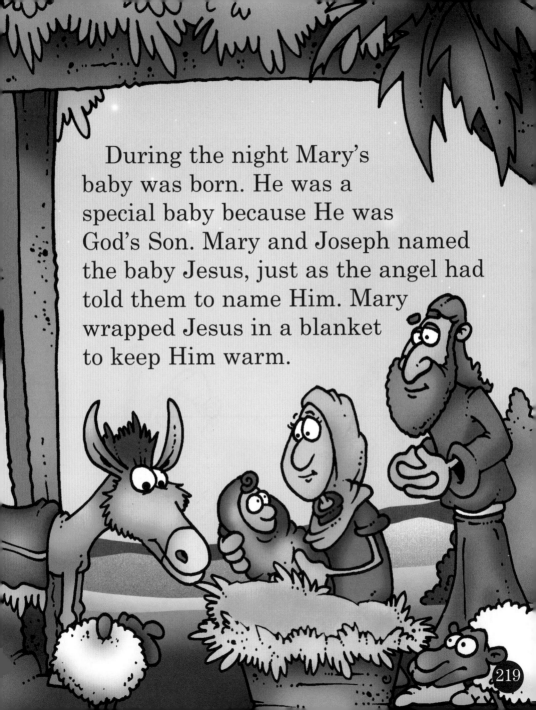

During the night Mary's baby was born. He was a special baby because He was God's Son. Mary and Joseph named the baby Jesus, just as the angel had told them to name Him. Mary wrapped Jesus in a blanket to keep Him warm.

Then Mary laid baby Jesus in a manger, the place that held hay for the animals to eat. A while later some shepherds peeked into the stable. "God sent an angel to tell us about this special baby," they said. "Can we see Him?"

The shepherds saw baby Jesus and
loved Him right away. They left the
stable and went to tell other people
about the special baby. Mary and Joseph
loved baby Jesus, too. They would take
good care of Him. Mary had quiet
thoughts about her very special baby.

221

Following the Star

Matthew 2

When Jesus was born a special star appeared in the sky. Some wise men who lived in a country far away saw it. They knew that the star was a sign that a new king had been born. The wise men wanted to see the new king.

They followed the star for a long time. It moved through the sky and led them to Jerusalem. The wise men talked to people in Jerusalem. "We are following a star," they said. "This star means that a new king was born. Do you know where He is now?" they asked.

When King Herod heard about a new king, he was angry. He did not want anyone else to be king. King Herod did not know that this new king was God's Son. He did not know that this king would be the ruler of heaven and earth.

Herod told the wise men, "When you find the new king, come back and tell me where He is. Then I can go see Him, too. I want to worship Him, too."

King Herod did not really want to worship the new king. He was trying to trick the wise men.

The wise men continued following the star. It led them right to the house where Jesus, Mary, and Joseph were staying. The wise men were happy to meet Jesus. They gave Him special gifts of gold, frankincense, and myrrh. They bowed down and worshiped Him.

Before they returned to their country, the wise men saw God in a dream. God told them that King Herod wanted to hurt Jesus. He told the wise men not to tell King Herod where Jesus lived. The wise men obeyed God and went home a different way.

Nighttime Escape

Matthew 2

King Herod had not forgotten the visit of the wise men. They had told him that a new king had been born. This new king would be king of the Jews. King Herod was not happy about that. He wanted to find the new king and kill Him. King Herod did not want anyone taking his job.

God knew that King Herod wanted to hurt Jesus. He sent an angel to Joseph in a dream. The angel said, "King Herod wants to hurt Jesus. You must run away right now. Take Jesus to Egypt. Stay there until I tell you it is safe to return."

Joseph quickly woke Mary. They left in the middle of the night. They took Jesus to Egypt. They lived there until the angel came back to Joseph in another dream. "King Herod is dead. It is safe for you to go home now," the angel said.

Joseph and Mary moved back to Nazareth, where they had lived before Jesus was born. Joseph worked as a carpenter again. Jesus grew up in Nazareth.

The Boy Teacher

Luke 2

Each year Mary and Joseph went to Jerusalem for the Passover celebration. It was a special time to remember how God took care of His people when they were slaves in Egypt. When Jesus was twelve years old, something happened on this trip to Jerusalem.

The Passover celebration had ended. The road was full of people. Mary and Joseph began walking home to Nazareth with their family and friends. They thought Jesus was somewhere in the group, too.

Later Mary and Joseph looked for Jesus. They could not find Him. He was not walking with any of the people they checked with. They worried that Jesus was lost in Jerusalem. Mary and Joseph hurried back to the city to look for Jesus.

They searched for three days. They looked everywhere for Jesus. At last they found Him. He was in the temple talking with the elders. He was asking them questions. They were asking Him questions, too. The elders were amazed at how much He understood.

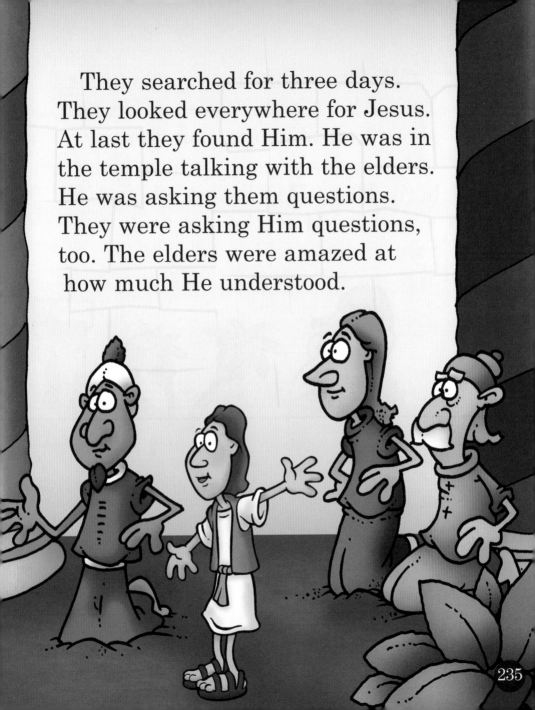

"We have looked everywhere for You," Mary said. "We were worried about You. Why did You do this?"

Jesus answered, "I had to come here. This is My Father's house. You should have known that I would be here."

Jesus enjoyed talking to the elders about God. He knew that God was His real Father. He was happy to share what He knew about God. But Jesus obeyed Mary and Joseph and went home with them.

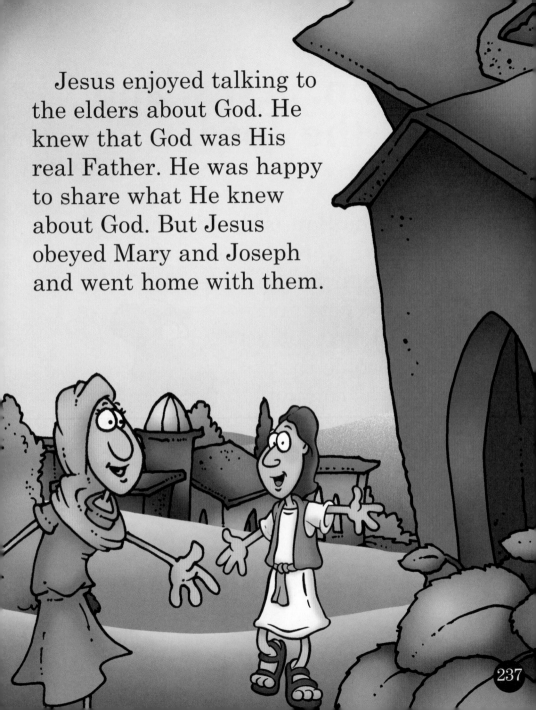

John, Jesus, and the Jordan

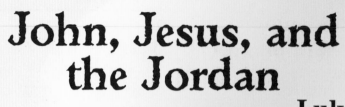

Luke 3

John the Baptist lived alone in the desert. He wore clothes made from camel's hair held by a leather belt. He ate locusts and honey. John's job was to tell people that Jesus was coming.

He told people that they were sinners.

"Stop sinning. Tell God you are sorry for your sins. Begin living with each other in a kinder way. Share what you have with those who do not have as much. Jesus, the Son of God, is coming soon." John wanted the people to be ready to listen to what Jesus told them.

When they heard John, many people decided to follow God. John baptized those people in the Jordan River. He dipped them under the water, then raised them up. That showed everyone their decision to follow God.

One day John was teaching about God near the Jordan River. Jesus came up and asked John to baptize Him. John knew that Jesus was God's Son. He said, "You should baptize me."

But Jesus wanted John to baptize Him. He knew that was the right way to do things. So He went out into the river. The people watched John baptize Jesus. When he lifted Jesus out of the water, something happened.

The sky opened up and God's Spirit came down. It looked like a dove flying through the sky. Everyone watched as it landed on Jesus. God's voice said, "You are My Son. I love You. I am very pleased with You."

Jesus' First Miracle

John 2

Jesus and His friends were invited to a wedding in a town called Cana. The celebration after the wedding went on for several days. The families of the couple made sure that the guests had plenty of good food to eat and wine to drink.

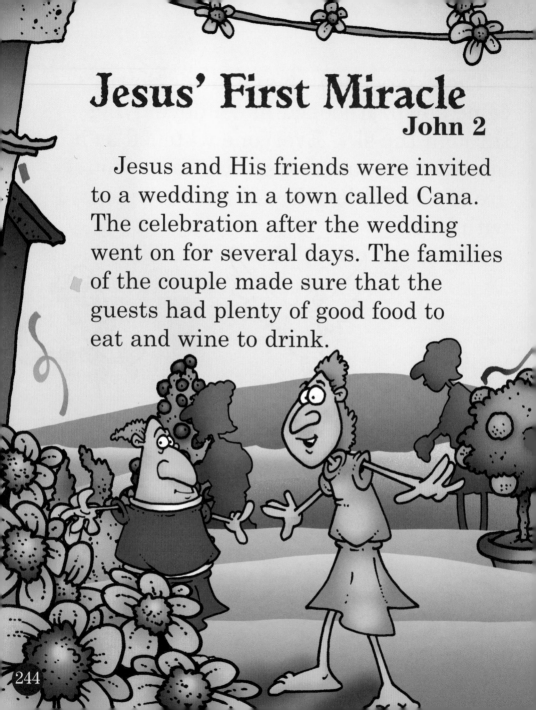

Mary, Jesus' mother, was at the wedding, too. In the middle of the celebration, she came to Him. "Our friends need help," she said. "They have run out of wine." Jesus told Mary that it was not time for Him to do miracles yet.

Still, Mary turned to the servants standing nearby. "Do whatever this man tells you to do," she said.

There were six big water jars in a corner. "Fill those jars with water," Jesus said. The servants did what He said.

"Now dip some out," He instructed. "Take it to the man who is in charge of the party." One servant reached into the jar and scooped some out. But it was not water anymore. It was wine now!

He took it to the host of the party and the man tasted it. "This is the best wine I have ever tasted."

He said to the man getting married, "Most people serve the best wine first. They serve cheaper wine later, when people are full. But you have saved the best wine for last."

The people at the party did not know that the wine had once been water. They did not know what Jesus had done. But the servants knew. This was Jesus' first miracle. This was the first time that He revealed the special powers God had given Him.

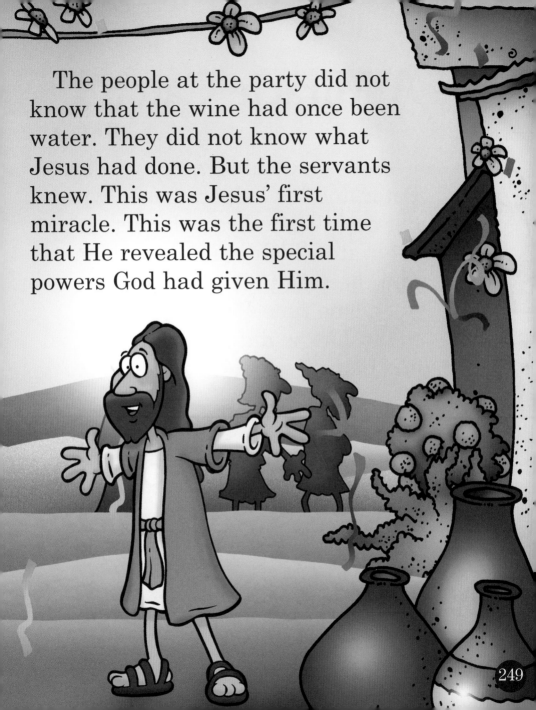

A Miracle Catch

Luke 5

Peter made his living by fishing. Peter and his helpers fished with big nets. They threw the nets into the water. Fish swam into them and the men pulled in the full nets. One time Peter fished all night, but he did not catch even one fish.

Peter and his friends came to shore the next morning. They were tired. But they had one more job to do before they could go home. They stretched the big fishing nets out on the shore. They had to wash the weeds and dirt off the nets. Then they would be ready to use the next time they fished.

Jesus was teaching nearby at the edge of a lake. Word spread that Jesus was there, and soon a big crowd gathered. People pushed to get close to Jesus. They wanted to be able to hear Him.

Jesus noticed the fishing boats on shore so He climbed into one. It was one of Peter's boats. Jesus asked Peter to row the boat out a little way from shore. Peter did. Jesus sat in the boat and taught the people. Peter listened.

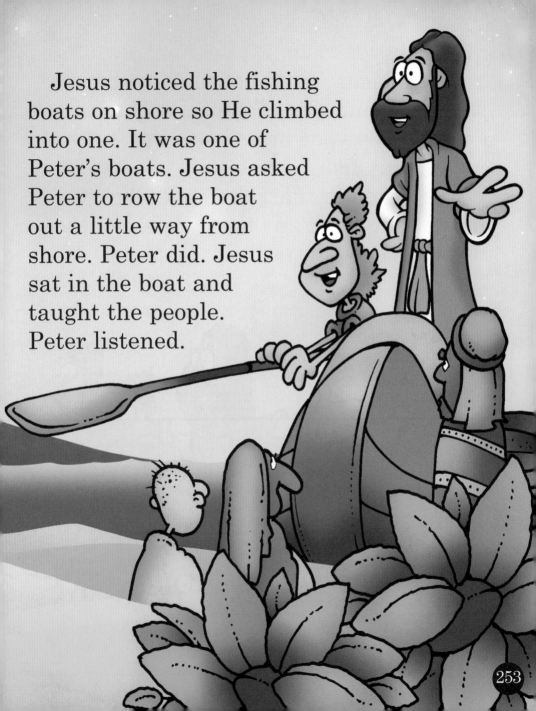

When Jesus was finished teaching, He pointed to one side of the boat. He said to Peter, "Drop your nets there. You will catch many fish."

"We fished in that very spot all night. We did not catch any fish," Peter said. But he obeyed Jesus.

Peter put the fishing nets into the water. They quickly filled up with many fish! They were so full that Peter had to call for help to pull them in. Now Peter understood that Jesus was sent from God. He fell to his knees.

"Do not be afraid," Jesus said. "From now on you will fish with Me. We will catch people for God."

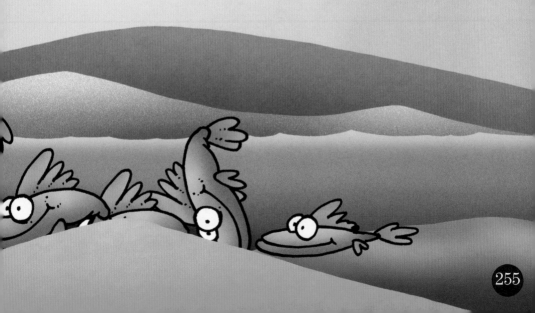

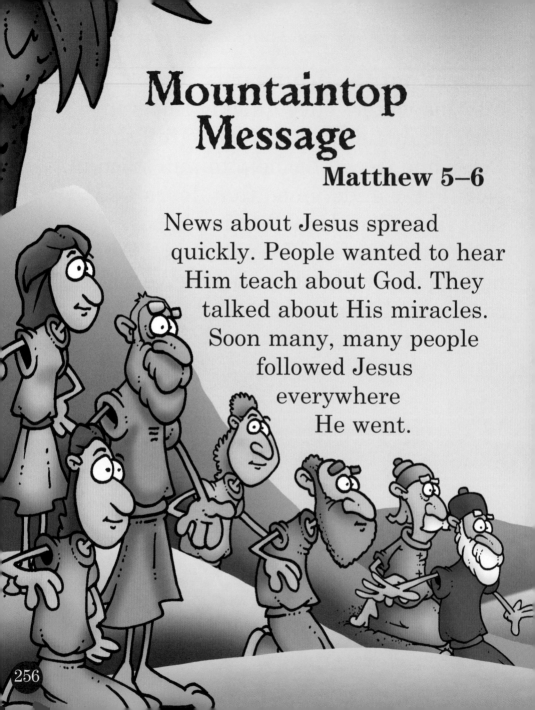

Mountaintop Message

Matthew 5–6

News about Jesus spread quickly. People wanted to hear Him teach about God. They talked about His miracles. Soon many, many people followed Jesus everywhere He went.

Some people stayed with Him all the time, learning about God. They were called disciples.

One day a crowd of people came to hear Jesus. He sat on the side of a mountain to teach. His disciples sat nearby and listened.

"You are the light of the world," Jesus said. "Do not hide your light under a basket. Let it shine for the whole world to see.

"The law of Moses says that you should not kill," He continued.

"I say that you should not even be angry with others. Love your enemies. Pray for those who are mean to you." The people listened to everything Jesus said.

"Do not put on a big show when you pray," Jesus taught. "When you pray, go off by yourself. Close the door and pray to your Father alone. Remember that He knows everything you need. He knows even before you ask Him.

"Build up treasures in heaven, not on earth. Do not worry about what you will wear. Do not worry about what you will eat or drink. Think about the birds. They do not worry about food. God takes care of them.

"Remember the flowers, too.
They do not have jobs. They
do not make clothes. But they
are more beautiful than even
a fancy king. You are more
important to God than birds
or flowers. So do not worry.
He will take care of you."

Four Good Friends

Mark 2

There was a crippled man who spent all day and all night in bed. This man had some good friends. Four of them were talking one day. "I wish we could do something to help our friend."

"Jesus is in town," said one. They had all heard about the wonderful miracles of Jesus.

The four men believed Jesus could heal their friend, so they came up with a good plan. They made a mat and put their crippled friend on it. They carried their friend across town to the house where Jesus was teaching.

The house where Jesus was teaching was crowded. The men could not take their friend inside. No one would let them through. But the friends did not give up. They made a new plan. They carried their friend up the stairs on the outside of the house.

They lowered their friend through
a hole in the roof. He was right in
front of Jesus! Jesus looked up at
them. He saw their faith in Him. He
looked down at the crippled man and
said, "Get up and walk." He did!
Everyone in the house was amazed.

A Rejoicing Mother

Luke 7

Everyone in town felt sad for a poor widow. Her husband had died some time before. All she had was her son. Then he died, too. Now the woman had no family at all. Her friends and the people in town helped her plan the funeral for her son.

On the day of the funeral, the woman and her friends were walking to the cemetery outside of town. Some men were carrying the dead young man's coffin on their shoulders. Everyone was very sad.

As they got to the town gate, there were some people coming into the city. Those people stepped aside to let the funeral pass by. They saw the sad mother. They heard her crying. They were quiet and respectful of her grief.

Jesus and His friends were in that crowd of people. Jesus saw the coffin. He could see how upset the mother was. He felt sad for her. Jesus wanted to do something to help her.

"Do not cry!" Jesus said to the mother. He walked over to the men who were carrying the young man's coffin. He touched the coffin. The men stopped. The people all watched Jesus. Everyone stood still.

Then Jesus said, "Young man, get up!" The young man sat up! He started talking to all those around him. The crowd of people did not know what to think! They were amazed at what Jesus could do.

Be Still!

Mark 4; Luke 8

A crowd of people came to hear Jesus teach. They sat quietly beside a lake listening to Him all day. It had been a long day and Jesus was tired. When He finished teaching He said, "Let's go across the lake."

Jesus and His friends got into a small boat and started across the lake. Jesus went right into the boat and fell asleep. The little boat rocked gently on the waves. The disciples let Jesus rest.

But when they were out in the middle of the lake, the wind got stronger. Waves splashed into the boat. The little boat bounced around in the water. The waves tossed it high into the air. Then it crashed back down into the water.

The disciples were afraid their boat would sink. Everyone was afraid except Jesus. He was still asleep. He did not even notice the water in the boat. He did not know about the big storm.

Finally, His friends got so scared that they woke Him up. "Jesus! Help us! Listen to the wind blowing. Look at the water splashing into our boat. We may die out here. Don't You care if we drown?"

"Why are you afraid?" He asked. Then He looked at the stormy sea.

"Be still!" He said. The storm stopped right away. Everything was quiet and still. Jesus' friends were amazed. Even the wind and the waves obeyed Him!

A Father's Faith

Matthew 9

Jairus was an important man in
the temple. He was used to giving
orders. He was used to people doing
what he said. But when his little girl
got sick, there was nothing Jairus
could do. Doctors took care of her,
but they could not make her well.

Jairus had heard about Jesus. He knew that Jesus healed sick people. Jairus wanted to ask Jesus to help his daughter. He hurried to find Jesus. He did not want his daughter to die.

Jairus did find Jesus. But he could not talk to Him right away. Jesus was helping someone else. Jairus worried as he waited until Jesus was free. Just as he began telling Jesus about his daughter, one of his servants came up.

"Your little girl is dead," the servant said. "Do not bother Jesus now." Jairus was very sad. He loved his little girl very much. His heart ached as he turned to leave. Jesus stopped him and said, "Do not worry."

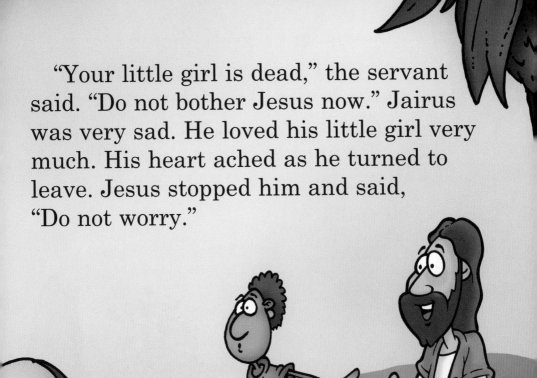

Jesus went to the home of Jairus. There were many people in the house. They were crying and talking about the little girl.

"Do not cry," Jesus said. "The little girl is not dead. She is just sleeping."

All of the people laughed at Jesus. They thought He was crazy. He sent all the people away except the little girl's mother and father, and three of His disciples. Then He went to the girl and said, "Get up." She did! Jairus and his wife were so happy when she did!

The True Neighbor

Luke 10

A man asked Jesus an interesting question. He said, "I know that I should love my neighbor. But just exactly who is my neighbor?" Jesus told him a story to help him understand who his neighbor was.

"A Jewish man was walking down a road. Some men beat him up, and stole his money and clothes. They left him lying on the road. The poor man was there for a long time. Finally, a Jewish priest from the temple came by. He crossed the road to get away from the hurt man.

"A little while later a temple worker came by. He looked at the man lying on the road. He could see that the man was hurt. But he did not want to help. In fact, he crossed the road to get away from the hurt man.

"Some time later a third man came by. This man was from Samaria. People from his country did not like Jewish people. But this man was kind. He stopped to check on the hurt man.

"The Samaritan put bandages on the hurt man. He put him on his donkey and took him to an inn. He paid the innkeeper to take care of him. He told the innkeeper to let the man stay as long as he needed. The kind man would pay all the bills."

Jesus finished the story. He asked the man which person in the story acted like a neighbor. The man said that the one who helped the hurt man was the neighbor. The man learned that his neighbor was anyone who needed his help.

A Miracle Picnic

Mark 6

Jesus went to a new town. He sat down and started teaching. A few people gathered around to hear Him. Then a few more came. Word spread through town that Jesus was teaching. More and more people came.

Soon there were thousands of people sitting on the hillside. They listened to Jesus teach all day.

When it got to be late in the day, some of His disciples said, "Send the people away so they can eat." But Jesus had another idea. He said, "Give them something to eat."

"We do not have any food. We do not have any money to buy food, either," one disciple said.

"I did see one little boy who brought a lunch," another one said. "He has five loaves of bread and two fish. That is not enough to feed all these people."

The little boy agreed to share his lunch with Jesus. "Tell the people to sit down," Jesus said. When everyone was sitting, He thanked God for the little boy's lunch.

He broke the bread and fish into pieces. He gave it to the disciples to pass out to the people. There was still more! Those few pieces became more and more pieces of bread and fish. More than 5,000 people had all they wanted to eat that day.

Jesus waited until everyone was full. Then He told His disciples to pick up the leftovers. They picked up twelve baskets of leftover food. All that food had come from one little boy's lunch!

Getting Out
of the Boat

Matthew 14

Jesus had been teaching all day. He
needed to be alone for a while. So He told
His disciples to get into their boat and go
across the lake. When the
disciples were on their
way, Jesus went up into
the hills to pray.

Sometime during the night the wind got strong. The disciples were having a hard time. They were rowing as hard as they could. But they were not making any progress. The wind was blowing their little boat backward.

Jesus saw that the disciples were having trouble. He came to help them. He walked to them on top of the water! The disciples saw something out on the water. In the dark they could not tell what it was. They were 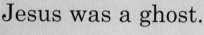 afraid because they thought Jesus was a ghost.

Jesus knew they were afraid. He called out to them. "Do not be afraid. It is I."

The disciple named Peter needed proof that it was really Jesus. "If it really is You, let me come to You on top of the water."

"Come," Jesus said. Peter hopped out of the boat and started walking on the water.

The other disciples watched Peter.
Everything was fine until Peter looked
around at the waves. He felt
the wind blowing in his face.
Suddenly he realized that he
was walking on water!
Slowly he started to sink.

"Help me!" he shouted. "Jesus, save me!" Jesus reached out His hand and pulled Peter out of the water. They both climbed into the boat and the wind stopped blowing. Everyone in the boat praised God. They believed Jesus was God's Son.

A Secret Touch

Matthew 9

Crowds of people surrounded Jesus as He walked down the road. Everyone wanted to be close to Him. People pushed and shoved to be near Him. Some people were just nosy. They wanted to see what He looked like. Others wanted to talk to Him. Some wanted Him to do things for them.

One lonely woman followed along at the back of the crowd. She had been sick for a long, long time. She had spent every cent she had going to doctors. None of them could make her better. She was very tired of being sick.

She thought that if she could just touch Jesus' clothes, she would get well. Bravely, she bent down and stretched her arm through the crowd of legs. She pushed through the crowd, reaching and stretching. Finally, she felt her fingers touch the edge of Jesus' robe.

Suddenly, Jesus stopped. "Who touched Me?" He asked. His disciples looked at one another in amazement. They wondered how Jesus could ask such a question. There were so many people around Him that lots of people had touched Him!

Jesus said to them, "I felt some power go out from Me. I know that someone touched Me for a special reason." He stopped right there on the road. He waited for the person who had touched Him to come forward.

The woman could hardly speak. She knew that she had been healed the minute she touched Jesus. Slowly she walked to Him. "I touched You," she said. She told Him her whole story. "You are well now because you believed," Jesus said. "Go in peace."

Two Sisters

Luke 10

Mary and Martha lived in
Bethany. They were friends with
Jesus. When He came to town He
stopped to see them. Mary and
Martha were sisters, but they
were not much alike.

The first time Jesus stayed with the sisters, Martha invited Jesus in. Then she got right to work. She cleaned the house. She started to cook a nice dinner to serve Jesus. Martha wanted every little thing to be just right.

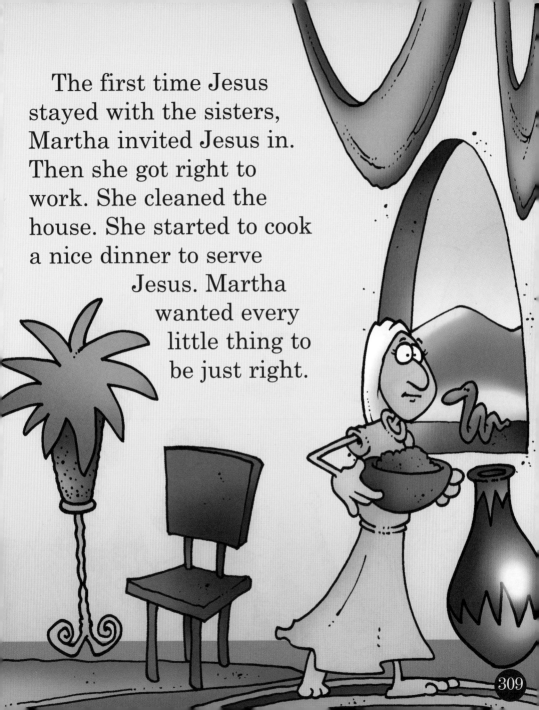

Martha worked and worked. She wanted it to be nice for Jesus. She had to finish making dinner. But Mary sat right down beside Jesus. He talked and Mary listened to everything He said.

Martha stirred the food. She was very busy and wished Mary would help her. But Mary was listening to Jesus. Martha chopped and cut. Mary still did not come. She was still sitting beside Jesus.

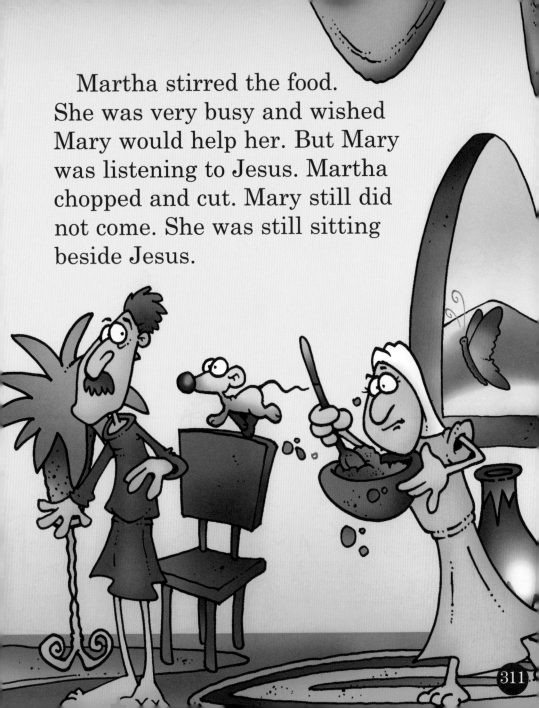

Martha worked a little longer. Finally, she could not take it anymore. She marched in to Jesus. "Tell Mary to come and help me!" she said. "I am doing all the work by myself. Mary should come and help me!"

"Martha," Jesus said, "you are worrying about many things. But Mary made the best choice. She is listening to Me. That is more important than anything else. Mary has discovered this truth."

Just Believe

John 11

Mary and Martha lived in Bethany with their brother, Lazarus. One day Lazarus became sick. His sisters took good care of him. But he got worse and worse. Finally, they sent for their friend, Jesus. They knew that He could make their brother well.

Several days passed and Jesus did not come. Lazarus got sicker and sicker until he finally died. Many friends sat with Mary and Martha. Everyone missed Lazarus. Days later, someone called, "Jesus is coming!" Mary wondered why He was coming now, when it was too late.

Martha ran out to meet Jesus. "If You had been here, my brother would not have died," she said. Later Mary ran out to see Jesus. She fell at his feet and cried. "If You had been here my brother would not have died," she said.

"I am the resurrection and the life," Jesus said. "Those who believe in Me may die, but they will live again." He turned to some men and ordered, "Open the tomb of Lazarus." They rolled the stone away from the door. "Lazarus, come out!" Jesus called. Mary and Martha stared as their brother walked out. He was alive!

A Father's Love

Luke 15

Jesus told this story: "Once there was a man who lived on a farm with his two sons. One day the younger son came to his father and said, 'Give me my share of your money and land now. I do not want to wait until you die.'

"The father agreed to divide up his money and give the younger son half of it. The son packed up his clothes and left for a country that was far away from his home.

319

"He spent his money on wild living in that faraway place. He did whatever he wanted to do. He did not think about how much money he was spending.

"Soon his money was all gone. He could not buy whatever he wanted now. In fact, he could not even buy food. He was alone, and he was far from home. He had nothing now.

"The only job the boy could find was on a pig farm. As he fed the pigs, he remembered his father's farm. The hired men on his father's farm lived better than he did now. Maybe he could go home and ask his father for a job. He felt that he did not deserve to be called his son anymore.

"He walked home. But before he reached his father's house, his father saw him coming and ran to meet him. He was so happy that his son was home that he threw a big party for him."

God is like the father in this story. He is always happy when people come back to Him.

Time for Children

Matthew 19

Some children skipped down the road ahead of their parents. Mothers carried little babies in their arms. Fathers carried young boys and girls on their shoulders. They were on their way to see Jesus.

All the parents and children were excited to get to see Jesus. Maybe they would even get to touch Him! Maybe He would bless them and pray for them. But when they got to the place where Jesus was, they got bad news.

"You cannot see Jesus," some of His helpers said. "He is too busy to talk to children. He has important things to do. Do not let the children bother Him." The parents and children thought that they would never meet Jesus now.

But Jesus heard what His helpers said. "Wait! Do not send the children away," He said. Jesus talked with the children. He held them. He blessed them. Jesus reminded everyone that the faith of children is strong. He said everyone should have faith like that.

A New Friend

Luke 19

Zacchaeus did not have many friends. He was a tax collector and he often cheated people. He took more money from them than he was supposed to take. That is why no one liked him.

One day Zacchaeus heard
that Jesus was coming through town.
A crowd of people quickly gathered.
Everyone wanted to see Jesus. Zacchaeus
wanted to see Him, too. But he had a
problem. He was at the back of
the crowd and he was too short to
see over the people.

No one would move for Zacchaeus. Then Zacchaeus had an idea. He ran ahead and climbed up a tall tree that was by the road. He scooted out on a branch. Now he had the perfect place to see Jesus going by. He could see everything.

When Jesus passed by the tree, He looked up at Zacchaeus. "Quick, come down, Zacchaeus," He said. "I want to come to your house today." Zacchaeus could not believe it. The people on the ground could not believe it, either.

Zacchaeus hurried down. He took Jesus to his house. At his home, he said, "I want to do the right thing. I will give half of all my money to the poor. And I will give back the money I took from people. In fact, I will pay them even more than I owe them."

That day Zacchaeus became a different man. He was not a mean man anymore. Now he was honest and kind. Jesus helped Zacchaeus to change. Now Zacchaeus believed Jesus was the Son of God.

A Woman's Big Gift

Mark 12

One day Jesus was in the temple.
He watched people give their
offerings. He saw rich people
with fancy clothes come
to the offering box.
They made a lot of
noise putting their
coins in. They gave
a lot of money.

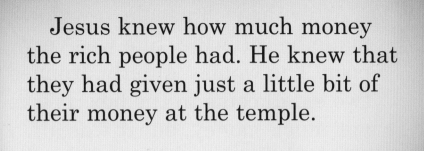

Jesus knew how much money the rich people had. He knew that they had given just a little bit of their money at the temple.

After the rich people, a widow made her offering. She was very poor. The woman quietly dropped two small coins in the box. It was not much money, but it was all she had. She wanted to give it for God's work.

Jesus talked to His disciples about the rich people and the widow. He said, "This widow gave more than all the others. They gave a tiny part of their money, but she gave all she had."

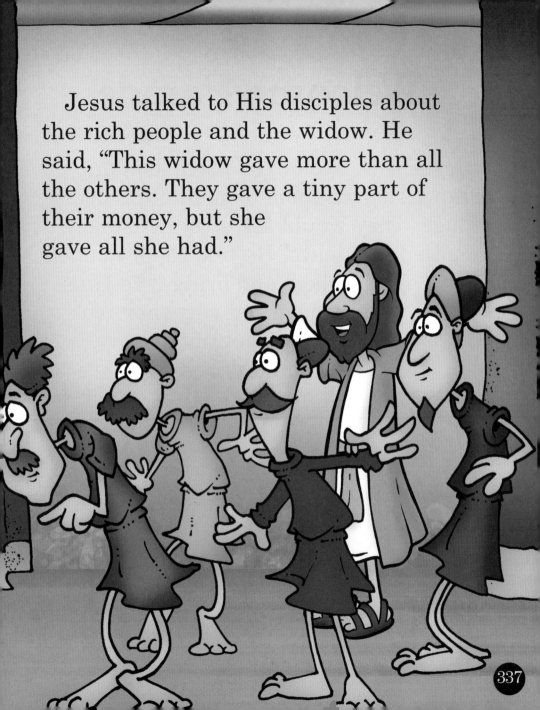

Welcome Parade

Matthew 21

Jesus sent two of His friends on an errand. He told them to go into the nearby village. They would see a young donkey tied to a fence. He told them to untie the donkey and bring it to Him. If anyone asked why they took the donkey, they should say, "The Lord needs it."

The two men hurried into town. Sure enough, they found a donkey, just as Jesus had told them. It looked like an ordinary donkey. But this donkey was special. Jesus was going to ride on its back into Jerusalem.

Jesus went into Jerusalem, even though He knew some leaders in the synagogue were angry. They did not want the people to like Jesus so much. They wanted people to listen to them instead. The leaders would arrest Jesus if they could.

The people watched Jesus coming down the road. "Hosanna!" they shouted. "Blessed is the King who comes in the name of the Lord!" The disciples joined in and shouted praises to God.

Some people cut branches off the palm trees and waved them in the air with excitement. Some people laid the branches down on the dusty road for the donkey to walk on.

Other people put their coats on the ground for the donkey to walk on. The crowd followed Jesus through the city gates. They cheered for Him.

A Special Dinner with Friends

Matthew 26

One evening Jesus and His twelve friends went to a room in the upstairs of a house. They ate the Passover supper together. Passover was an important celebration to the Jewish people.

While they were eating, Jesus said, "One of you is planning to do something that will hurt Me."

His friends did not understand what He was talking about.

"Are You talking about me? Is it me?" One by one each man asked if he was the one Jesus was talking about.

Jesus quietly said, "One of you will betray Me. The Scriptures said long ago that the Son of Man must die. And the time has come for that to happen."

The disciples stared at one another, wondering which one it would be.

Then Judas said, "It isn't me, is it?" Jesus looked right at him and answered, "Yes, Judas, it is you." Judas ran out of the room. The other disciples did not understand what was happening.

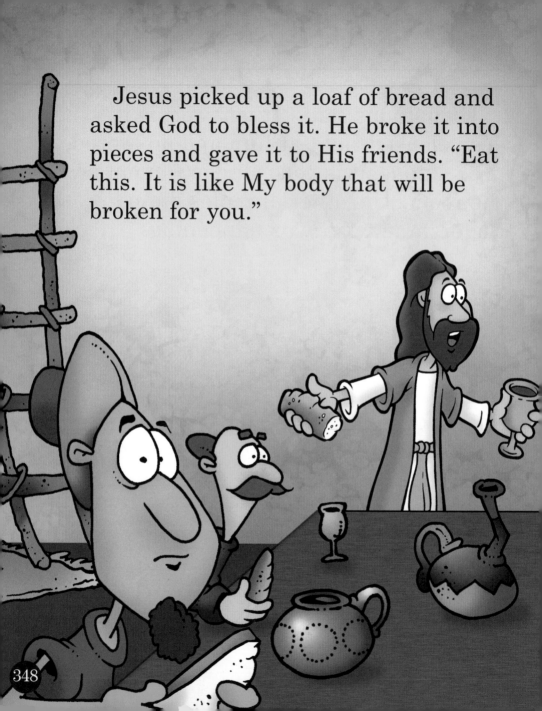

Jesus picked up a loaf of bread and asked God to bless it. He broke it into pieces and gave it to His friends. "Eat this. It is like My body that will be broken for you."

He picked up the cup of wine and thanked God for it. "Drink this," He said to the disciples. "It is like My blood that will be spilled for you. These things will happen to Me so that the sins of many people can be forgiven."

In the Garden

Matthew 26

After the Passover supper, Jesus took His friends to a garden. He wanted to spend some time praying. He wanted His friends to pray, too. He left them and went ahead of them.

Jesus fell to the ground. He told God that He did not really want to go through the hard things that were coming. He asked God to stop them. But then He prayed, "I will do whatever You want."

Jesus thought His disciples were praying, too. But when He returned to them, He saw that each man had fallen asleep. Jesus was sad that they did not understand how much He wanted them to pray.

"Wake up!" He said. "Pray with Me!"

Jesus went to pray again. He prayed so hard that drops of sweat that looked like blood dripped from His face. His friends tried to stay awake and pray, but they fell asleep again. Jesus went to check on them just as Judas and a group of soldiers came into the garden.

Unbelievable!

Matthew 26

The time was quickly coming when Jesus would die. His death was part of God's plan to help people be able to go to heaven someday. God planned that Jesus would die for the sins of all people.

Judas led some soldiers into the garden where Jesus was praying. The Hebrew leaders had paid Judas thirty pieces of silver to show the soldiers which man was Jesus. The soldiers could then bring Him to the Hebrew leaders.

Judas walked up to Jesus and kissed His cheek. That was the sign the soldiers were waiting for. The soldiers surrounded Jesus. Some of them grabbed Him. He did not try to run away. He did not even move. The soldiers arrested Him.

Peter, one of Jesus'
disciples, wanted to protect
Jesus. He pulled out a sword
and cut off one soldier's ear.
"Stop!" Jesus shouted. He told
His friend to put the sword away.

Then Jesus touched the soldier's ear. It was healed! It looked as good as new. The disciples could not believe that Jesus would heal the soldier's ear.

The soldiers took Jesus out
of the garden to meet with the
Hebrew leaders. The disciples were scared
and ran away. Judas ran away, too. He
was sorry that he had helped the soldiers
find Jesus. But it was too late. Judas
could not change things now.

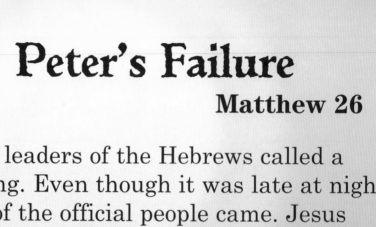

Peter's Failure

Matthew 26

The leaders of the Hebrews called a meeting. Even though it was late at night most of the official people came. Jesus stood in front of them while they accused Him of things that were not true.

Peter followed far behind the soldiers. He wanted to see what happened to Jesus. But he did not want anyone to know that he was Jesus' friend. He stood outside the building where the leaders were meeting. He warmed his hands over a fire.

"You are a friend of Jesus," a girl said. She said it so loudly that others heard her. Peter was afraid. "What are you talking about? I do not know Him!" Peter shouted.

A little while later another girl pointed at Peter. "You were with Jesus!" she said. "I saw you with Him." Again Peter shouted, "Leave me alone. I do not know Him!"

Later, another person said, "You are a stranger in Jerusalem. You must be one of Jesus' followers." Now Peter was very scared. "Once and for all, I'm telling you that I do not know that man!" he shouted. Just then Peter heard a rooster crow.

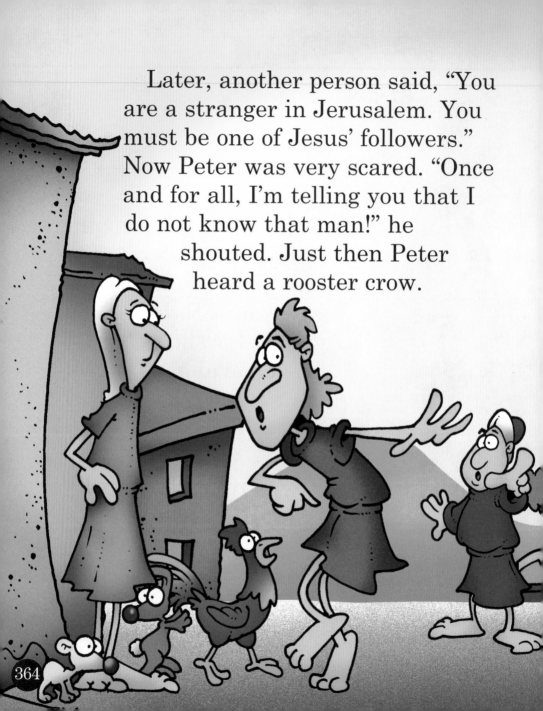

Peter remembered what Jesus had said earlier that day. Peter had bragged about how much he loved Jesus. "Before the first rooster crows, you will say three times that you do not even know Me," Jesus had said. Now Peter walked away, crying hard.

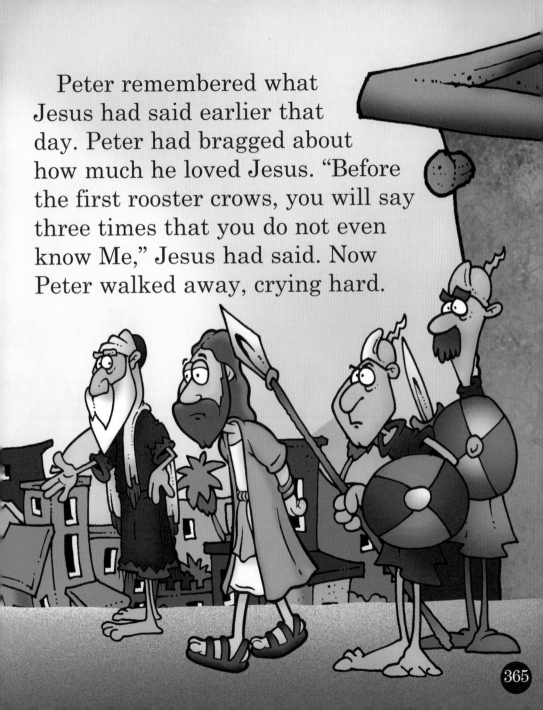

Crucify Him!

Matthew 27

Jesus said that He was the Son of God. That made the leaders of the Hebrew people so angry that they wanted to kill Him. They took Him to Pilate, the Roman governor.

Pilate could order Jesus' death. Crowds of people came to hear what Pilate would say about Jesus. Pilate said, "I do not see that Jesus has done anything wrong. It is my custom to free one prisoner during the Passover season."

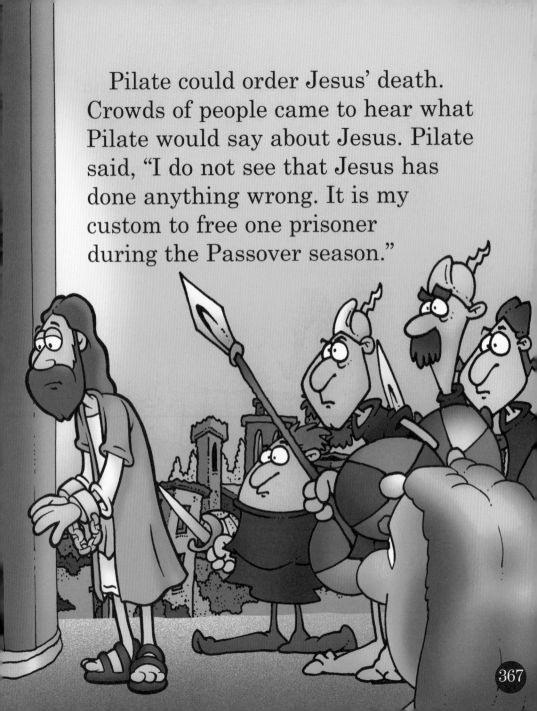

"I will release Jesus or the criminal named Barabbas. Which one do you want?"

"We want Barabbas!" the people shouted.

"What about Jesus?" Pilate asked.

"Crucify Him!" the crowds shouted.

The soldiers put a crown of thorns on His head and a purple robe on His body. Then they spat at Him and made fun of Him. "Hail, King of the Jews!" they said. They even hit Him with a stick.

Then the soldiers put a big wooden cross on Jesus' back. It was the cross that He would die on. They made Him carry it to the hill outside of town.

A crowd of people followed Jesus through town to the hill. Some of Jesus' friends were in the crowd, too. They felt very sad because of the things happening to Jesus.

The Saddest Day
Luke 23

The soldiers led Jesus to the hill outside of town that was called Golgotha, where they crucified criminals. They nailed Jesus' hands and feet to the big cross and then raised it.

Two thieves were also being crucified that day. They were on crosses on each side of Jesus. People stood around the crosses watching the men die. Some of them made fun of Jesus. They shouted, "Hey, if You are really God's Son, why don't You call for some angels to help You?"

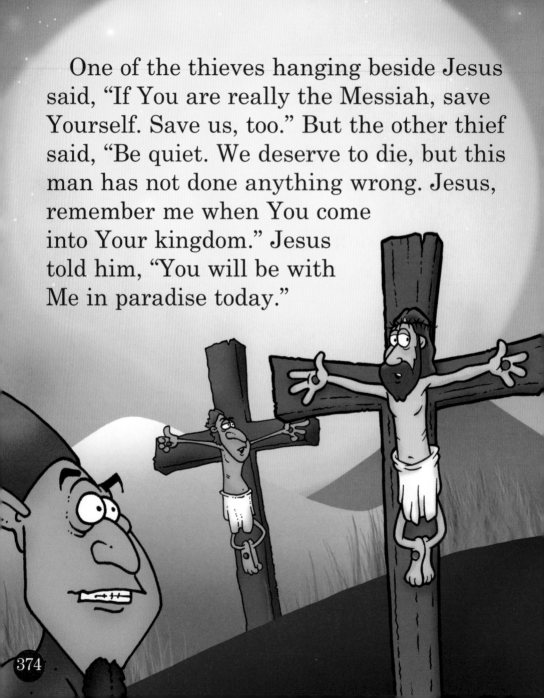

One of the thieves hanging beside Jesus said, "If You are really the Messiah, save Yourself. Save us, too." But the other thief said, "Be quiet. We deserve to die, but this man has not done anything wrong. Jesus, remember me when You come into Your kingdom." Jesus told him, "You will be with Me in paradise today."

"He saved others but not Himself!" the Hebrew leaders shouted. Jesus said, "Father, forgive these people. They do not know what they are doing." By noon Jesus was getting close to death. Suddenly the sky was very dark and for about three hours it was as dark as night. Then Jesus said, "Father, I give My Spirit into Your hands." Then Jesus died.

Jesus died on the cross so that people's sins would be forgiven. He did that because He loved us so much. This was God's plan so that people could be in heaven with Him someday.

Jesus' friends took His body down from the cross. They took Jesus to a cave and laid Him there. Soldiers rolled a big stone in front of the cave door. Other soldiers guarded it so that no one could steal Jesus' body.

A Joyful Morning

Matthew 28

Early on Sunday morning some women set out for Jesus' cave. They were Jesus' friends. They were taking oils and perfumes to put on His body. That was what people did in those days.

As they walked through the garden, the women talked about the big stone. "How are we going to move that stone?" they wondered. "It is so big that it took many soldiers to put it in place."

Suddenly they heard a big rumble. It was like an earthquake. Then they saw something amazing. The stone was gone! An angel was standing in the doorway. Now they knew what the big noise had been.

"I know you are looking for Jesus. He is not here," the angel said. "He came back to life! Just like He said He would!" The women ran back to tell others the good news.

Seeing Is Believing

John 20

Jesus' friends were together in a room. They kept the door locked because the leaders of the Hebrew people were angry. They thought someone had stolen Jesus' body from the tomb. Suddenly Jesus was in the room with them. "Peace be with you!" He said. He talked with them and then left.

But one disciple, Thomas, had not been in that room when Jesus came. He would not believe that Jesus was really alive. "How can He be alive again?" he argued. No one could make Thomas believe that Jesus was alive.

A week later, Thomas and more of Jesus' friends were in a room together. Suddenly Jesus was standing in the room with them, even though the door was locked! Jesus went to Thomas. He showed him the nail holes in His hands. He let Thomas touch His hands.

Now Thomas believed that Jesus was really alive. "You have seen Me, so you believe," Jesus said. "Blessed are the people who have not seen Me and still believe."

Homeward Bound

Acts 1

Jesus and His friends were in Jerusalem together after He had risen from the dead. He taught them more about God. They listened closely. They wanted to hear everything He said. Now they knew for sure that He was God's Son.

"Tell people all over the world about Me," Jesus said. Then He disappeared into the sky. A cloud covered Him so they could not see Him anymore. Jesus' friends stood looking up into the sky for a long time.

Suddenly two angels stood beside them. "Why are you looking at the sky?" they asked. "Jesus has gone to heaven. Someday He will come back the same way that you saw Him leave."

Jesus' friends remembered the things that He had taught them. They knew that Jesus was in heaven making a place for them. They went back to Jerusalem together. They spent lots of time together praying.

Flames of Spirit

Acts 2

After Jesus rose from the dead, He talked with His friends many times. One time He told them to wait in Jerusalem until He sent them the gift. They did what Jesus told them to do. They wanted to obey Him.

On the day of Pentecost, a Jewish holiday seven weeks after Passover, all of Jesus' friends were gathered in a room. They were celebrating Pentecost together. Suddenly a loud noise filled the room. It sounded like a powerful windstorm.

The people looked around, but could not figure out where the sound was coming from. As the sound of the roaring wind continued, little flames appeared in the air. The flames blew around the room and settled above each person's head. This was the gift Jesus had promised them! It was the presence of the Holy Spirit!

The Spirit of God filled each person and they began to speak in languages they did not even know. People from other nations who were living in Jerusalem heard about what was happening. They ran to the room and heard their own languages being spoken. It was amazing! Many people began to believe in Jesus that day.

The Future
Looks Good

John was one of Jesus' closest friends. He spent his life telling people about Jesus. Some leaders did not like that, so they sent John away. He lived alone on an island. There was no one there to hear him talk about Jesus.

One day John had a dream.
He heard a voice that was as loud
as a trumpet blowing. He turned
around and saw Jesus!
But Jesus did not look
like He used to look.
His body was
glowing like
the sun.

"Do not be afraid," Jesus said. "I am going to show you things about the future. Write everything down so all people will know what is going to happen someday."

John saw the doorway to
heaven open up. He saw God sitting
on His throne. A beautiful rainbow
was all around it. Angels surrounded
the throne. They were all praising God.
It was a beautiful sight.

Then John saw a new city. The light of God was everywhere. It was a beautiful place. God was preparing this place for people who love Him. Someday all Christians would be together with Him in heaven.

Heaven

John saw that the devil and his helpers would be punished for the bad things they had done on earth. In heaven there would be no more pain. There would be no death and no crying. Jesus told John, "I am coming soon for My people."

John said, "Come, Lord Jesus. Amen."